STATE OF MINDS

Charles N. Prothro Texana Series

Original manuscript page from "The Pits."

State of Minds

TEXAS CULTURE AND ITS DISCONTENTS

Don Graham

 UNIVERSITY OF TEXAS PRESS
Austin

Requests for permission to reproduce material from this
work should be sent to:
    Permissions
    University of Texas Press
    P.O. Box 7819
    Austin, TX 78713-7819
    www.utexas.edu/utpress/about/bpermission.html
♾ The paper used in this book meets the minimum
requirements of ANSI/NISO Z39.48-1992 (R1997)
(Permanence of Paper).

LIBRARY OF CONGRESS CATALOGING-IN-PUBLICATION DATA
Graham, Don
State of minds : Texas culture and its discontents /
Don Graham. — 1st ed.
p. cm.   —   (Charles N. Prothro Texana series)
Includes bibliographical references.
ISBN 978-0-292-72361-0 (cloth : alk. paper)
1. American literature—Texas—History and criticism.
2. Texas—In literature.   3. Texas—Intellectual life.
4. Texas—In motion pictures.   I. Title.
PS266.T4G675   2011
810.9'32764—dc22

                                          2010026705

ISBN 978-0-292-73490-6 (E-book)

For Larry McMurtry and Betsy Berry

"Texas culture? That's an oxymoron, isn't it?" Among the discouraging words not infrequently heard on the University of Texas campus

"Texas culture": 116,000,000 sites on Google

WOULD APPRECIATE ARTICLE ON TEXAS AS BACKGROUNDER JOHNSON STOP COWBOYS COMMA OIL COMMA MILLIONAIRES COMMA HUGE RANCHES COMMA GENERAL CRASSNESS COMMA BAD MANNERS ETC.
—CABLE FROM BRITISH EDITOR TO ALISTAIR COOKE, 1968

"I am ready to tell the world that Texas is a paradise for lovers of the avant-garde, and Houston is what the French like to dub on their signposts a "ville d'art."
—MARTIN GAYLORD, "SPACE AND LIGHT IN TEXAS," *THE SPECTATOR*, FEBRUARY 27, 2004

"I was immersed in Texas' culture . . ."
—SEN. HILLARY CLINTON, "WHAT TEXAS MEANS TO ME," *THE TEXAS OBSERVER*, FEBRUARY 22, 2008

TABLE OF CONTENTS

ACKNOWLEDGMENTS

Since faculty leaves are hard to come by these days, I am especially grateful to Randy L. Diehl, dean of the College of Liberal Arts at the University of Texas, for granting me a College Research Fellowship; and to Elizabeth Cullingford, chair of the Department of English, for vigorously supporting my candidacy. Time to think, study, and rewrite has made this book possible, and I thank them both for the opportunity.

I also want to thank my editors and fact-checkers at *Texas Monthly,* the magazine where many of these pieces originally appeared. First in order is Evan Smith, former editor of *Texas Monthly.* Evan was very supportive and always great at coming up with good ideas for columns and articles. Second is Quita McMath, who edited many of my columns. Quita's favorite word was "tweak," as in "Can you tweak this?" (to which the only answer was yes). With each new assignment I would strive to write the perfect, flawless column (approximately 1800–2000 words), and she would invariably have forty or so follow-up queries and suggestions. She made every column better, and I firmly believe that she would have asked Abe Lincoln to tweak the Gettysburg Address. Other editors who provided valuable help were Brian Sweany and Jake Silverstein. I also want to thank the fact-checkers, who were amiably relentless in their pursuit of factual accuracy. These include Pat Booker, Chester Rosson, John Spong, David Moorman, and Valerie Wright. John Broders, the gatekeeper, was also always very helpful. If there is something about *Texas Monthly* that Broders doesn't remember, then it's not worth remembering.

For their generosity in allowing me permission to reprint the pieces from *Texas Monthly,* I want to express my gratitude to Evan Smith, Cathy Casey, and Jake Silverstein.

As always, I consulted old friends and sw Lit scholars Tom Pilkington and Mark Busby, and as always, they came through with useful information. I also want to thank my colleagues Peter LaSalle and William J. Scheick for advice and support. I would like to thank Calli Rudebusch, a student in my sw Life & Lit Class in spring of 2010, for bringing the lbj-pants episode to my attention. Finally, I must thank "Reader No. 2," whose report on the manuscript to the University of Texas Press was helpful in my final thinking about what to include and what not to.

I also wish to thank Katie Salzmann, lead archivist of the Southwestern Writers Collection, for guiding me through the fascinating file on *No Country for Old Men* in the Cormac McCarthy Papers at the Southwestern Writers Collection, the Wittliff Collections, Texas State University—San Marcos.

The selection process was not always easy. During the decade spanned by this volume, nearly a hundred essays of mine on Texas literature, history, film, and culture were published. Fifty-three of those appeared in *Texas Monthly,* a number in *The Texas Observer,* and the rest in various journals and in edited books. The present collection reprints nineteen of that total, and I am grateful to all the editors who shepherded them into print and to those same editors for granting permission to reprint.

The acquisitions editor at the University of Texas Press, William Bishel, has been very helpful in all regards, and I am grateful to him, as I am to Dave Hamrick, assistant director and marketing and sales director, for their enthusiastic support.

I also want to thank Victoria Davis, manuscript editor, and Teri Sperry, copy editor, for their outstanding work on the manuscript.

Finally, I wish to thank my wife, Betsy Berry, who is a superb editor and thinker-up of titles. As always I am indebted to her for help in all areas of writing and living.

STATE OF MINDS

INTRODUCTION
The Ayes of Texas

Perhaps another state honors its writers more
than Texas, but if so I don't know which one. We have the
Texas Institute of Letters, the Texas Book Festival, Texas Writers
Month, the Writers' League of Texas, the Texas Literary Hall of
Fame, and uncounted books-and-authors events held in cities
from Amarillo to Beaumont.

We have statues of dead and living authors. The Dobie-
Bedichek-Webb installation at Zilker Park in Austin celebrates
the Texas Trio, and, odd but true, Sea World in San Antonio
sports a statue of Katherine Anne Porter. Texas State in San
Marcos boasts a statue of John Graves. A statue of the late Elmer
Kelton will soon be on view in San Angelo.

We have local shrines in little towns, avatars of the muse's
approbation. KAP's childhood home in Kyle is a National Historic
Site. In Rockdale the memory of George Sessions Perry is kept
green by an historical plaque, the library, and occasional talks by
visiting scholars. In little Cross Plains the little library has a special collection of books and memorabilia devoted to local star
Robert E. Howard of Conan the Barbarian fame.

And there is no paucity of centers. The University of North
Texas used to have a Center for Texas Studies, now TCU has one
with the same title; Texas State has a very active Center for the
Study of the Southwest (read Texas); SMU has one; and the University of Texas has the Michener Center for Writers, although
its purview is decidedly national. I'm sure I've left out a statue or
two, a center or two. And of course there is no dearth of schol-

arly writing on Texas literature or of courses in universities and colleges devoted to the study of that literature. Scholarship in the 1980s did a particularly good job of bringing to our attention the work of forgotten or overlooked women and minority writers, and that work continues. The full portrait of Texas literature in its multiplicity and, yes, complexity, is a work in progress.

I think the key to understanding all of this literary hullabaloo is that if Texans don't celebrate the writing of their native state, nobody else is going to. Examples of the general disparagement of Texas literary culture by outsiders are abundant. Here, for example, is an assessment of the presumptive tastes of Texas readers: "Even educated Texans have often preferred insubstantial humour books and western pulp fiction to 'highfalutin' writing." This little bit of condescension appeared in *The Economist* in 1998, in an article by an anonymous visitor to what he or she regarded as a distinct oddity: the Texas Book Festival. Imagine thousands of Texans gathering to listen to writers. Unthinkable.

If the audience is ridiculed, so are the writers. The jacket copy from a collection of stories titled *Southwest,* published by a New York house in the 1980s, caricatured its own selections: "Some were born among the sagebrush and the mesquite trees. Others traveled here from the soot-choked cities of the East. But all write with their feet dusty from the mesas or with fingers greasy from chicken-fried steak."

In foreign climes northeast of the Red River, there is still a hunger for the clichés and gaucheries that constitute our ignorant lives. Typical is a review by one Benjamin Moser that appeared in the *New York Review of Books* in May 2004. His piece is devoted to Larry McMurtry's Berrybender saga, but it's one of those reviews that casts a much bigger lariat. Mr. Moser writes of the "louche fictions" of *Giant* and *Dallas* (misusing the word *louche* in the process: it means shady, disreputable). Anyway, these "louche fictions," he opines, lead Texans to think of themselves as "flamboyant playboy millionaires." I think most Texans are just savvy enough to distinguish their lives from those depicted in movies or in television. Mr. Moser lives in a better, more cultivated place than the Houston where he says he grew up. He lives in the Netherlands, where, I can imagine, one never sees a surfeit of poppy paintings and windmill *objets* in the domiciles of Mr. Moser's neighborhood.

The fact is, Texas has done a much better job of exporting its mystique than it has its truths—aided and abetted, of course, by Yankee expectations. Annie Proulx, a New Englander, provides a good example of a recent caricature of Texas manners and mores in her 2002 novel, *That Old Ace in the Hole*. The book traces the erratic fortunes of 25-year-old Bob Dollar, who has been sent down to the Panhandle from the Denver office of Global Pork Rind to scout locations for new hog farms. He moves to a place improbably called Woolybucket, where he meets tons of people with names odder than his. Proulx's habit of giving characters eccentric names leads her to such extremes as Ribeye Cluke, Rope Butt, Harry Howdiboy, LaVon Fronk, Wally Ooly, Freda Beautyrooms, and Dick Head, among many, many others. Fanny Proustnot must never have heard of Ima Hogg, though there is mention of one Venus Hogg. In a single paragraph Nannie Pootluck gives us Hen Page, Cy Frease, and Coolbroth Fronk.

The other problem, and one that went unremarked upon in all the reviews I read, most of them by Yankees who wouldn't know any better, is Proulx's penchant for dialect, or what she might call "dilek." Thus "Granddaddy" becomes "Graindeddy," sometimes "Graindaddy," but never "Grandaddy" which is the way Texuns say it. "Homaseashells" is her most ridiculous stab at regional speech. She also thinks Texans say "crik." They do not. You have to go to Battle Crik, Michigan, to hear that.

It's not surprising that outsiders, distant observers, might well cast a superior eye on things Texan. But it is also the case that within Texas, especially within academic culture, there is considerable resistance to admitting that Texas possesses any sort of literary culture worth mentioning. Back in 1895, when pioneering folklorist John A. Lomax was getting his B.A. at the University of Texas, he showed a manuscript of cowboy songs to a senior professor in the English Department. In his autobiography Lomax described the professor's reaction: "Dr. Calloway told me that my samples of frontier literature were tawdry, cheap, and unworthy . . . There was no possible connection, he said, between the tall tales of Texas and the tall tales of *Beowulf.*" Lomax had to go to Harvard to find a professor who appreciated the great, inestimable value of those songs and urged their publication. The result, in 1910, was the groundbreaking *Cowboy Songs and Frontier Ballads.* Later on, J. Frank Dobie had to battle similar resistance by professors in the University of Texas English Department to the idea of developing a course in southwestern literature, but Dobie prevailed and that course, Life and Literature of the Southwest, is still offered.

The perception of Texas's uniqueness, and the concomitant fear that the state might lose that special identity, goes back at least to the Centennial Celebration of 1936. That year Dobie, already known as "Mr. Texas," published a collection of essays titled *The Flavor of Texas.* In the opening essay, "Flavor and Tradition," Dobie piled up colorful examples of the "Texas tradition." (Dobie used the word *tradition* instead of *culture,* but it was the same thing.) In one passage he addressed the dreaded prospect of change but managed to reach a consoling conclusion:

> The tendency of urban centers, machinery, constantly accumulating regulations over all industries, standardization of newspapers and education, and now all that the New Deal implies have been as active towards standardizing individuals in Texas as elsewhere over the United States. Nevertheless the tradition is still individualistic; the ideal is still against "swallering that."

By 1968, A. C. Greene felt more pessimistic about the prospect of Texas losing its indigenous culture, as he wrote in *A Personal Country:*

> This ability to identify so much with one's place of birth is becoming rare in American culture. I don't

think my children have it and I have not tried to give it to them. They have lived in places that didn't strike up through the soles of their feet or assault their eyeballs. If there are fewer of us who retain our identity with a region there are fewer regions powerful enough to force an identity. In our mobility and our conformity, in our ability to shape our physical circumstances and adapt nature to our convenience, we are losing sectionalism, not just in its less desirable ways but in its meaningful sense.

In the twenty-first century I find that students, very good students indeed, who enroll in my Life and Literature of the Southwest class (the one Dobie invented) do not know who Dobie was and have never heard the name except in relation to the Dobie Mall, a high-rise mixed-use building on the edge of the UT campus. I have observed the fading of Dobie's name from general awareness for going on twenty years, but more recently the number of students who have some inkling of who Dobie was has dropped to nil. But there is more news of slippage on the culture recognition front. Many of my students have never heard of Larry McMurtry either, or John Graves, the two best-known Texas writers of the modern era. Even more surprising, to me anyway, is that they have, by overwhelming numbers, never seen *Red River, Giant, Hud, The Last Picture Show,* or *Lonesome Dove*—all major texts in the definition and dissemination of what Texas used to be. The erosion of local knowledge in the past few decades has been pronounced.

It was Dobie himself who made the most eloquent case for the study of regional culture. In the essay "How My Life Took Its Turn" Dobie wrote:

> If people are to enjoy their own lives, they must be aware of the significances of their own environments. The mesquite is, objectively, as good and as beautiful as the Grecian acanthus. It is a great deal

better for people who live in the mesquite country. We in the Southwest shall be civilized when
the roadrunner as well as the nightingale has
connotations.

In view of Dobie's endorsement of the local, it is somehow
unfathomable to hear the most important Texas writer in the
state's history assert in an interview that "Texas itself doesn't
have anything to do with why I write. It never did." But it is
hard to imagine that anybody who has read *Horseman, Pass By*,
The Last Picture Show, In a Narrow Grave: Essays on Texas (note the
subtitle!), or his great cattle drive epic *Lonesome Dove* would
agree with Larry McMurtry on this score. But then perhaps
Larry was simply trying to escape the pejorative associations of
being considered only a Texas writer.

I am not so much interested in the material objects of Texas
culture—the kitsch, the little found poems (You'll do time / For
a Crime / in Grimes County—a sign greeting visitors to that
county), the phony idioms ("All hat and no cattle"), the Burnt-
Orange Long Horn Junque on sale all over Austin, Texas. My
interest is mainly in literary and film culture. Texas writing is a
subset of American literature, and the writers who interest me
the most are those who have found a way to hitch their narratives to a national star, while keeping in mind the Lone Star from
which their work originates.

All of this may change in the future. Tom Pilkington, a longtime and important scholar of Texas writing, has argued that the
very idea of a Texas literary tradition may be winding down.
Writes Pilkington, "As the American population becomes ever
more ethnically diverse, ever more mobile—ever more root-
less and transient—regional ties and loyalties are weakened or
obliterated. I do not foresee a Texas literary tradition, in anything like its twentieth-century form, surviving very far into the
twenty-first century." His point is that if Texas ceases to think of
itself as a nation-state, then the allure of the mystique will fade
away. I think the mystique will continue in the production of
consumer products and the rhetoric of politicians. But Pilking-

ton may well be right regarding a literary tradition headed for the barn. I am not nostalgic about this possibility. I have always loved great writing, wherever it comes from.

The present collection is a series of essays dealing with Texas-inflected books and authors. It spans a ten-year period, 1999–2009, and to my mind stands as a bookend to an earlier collection, *Giant Country: Essays on Texas* (TCU Press), published in 1998. Many of the pieces gathered here appeared originally in *Texas Monthly* as columns and were conceived of as opportunities for expanding the form beyond a book review format. This concept allowed me to connect many of the pieces with my own personal experiences growing up in Texas. Thus the reviews became occasions for observations, larger speculations, and commentary. Here I have taken the opportunity to revise, delete, add, and otherwise bring the material forward in time. Culture is always changing, never static, and the process of reading is always a process of rereading as well. Such a book asks of its audience only an interest in literature, history, and film, in this case Texas literature, history, and film.

PART I   *Texas*

LUCAS, TEXAS, LUCAS, TEXAS

The day I learned to write my name, in the first grade, I wrote it all over the windowsill and wall at the back of the schoolhouse where eight grades, one per row, studied grammar, history, spelling, geography, mathematics, and rudimentary social manners. I don't know why I scribbled my name a hundred times or more in that place, at that time. Perhaps it was just the elation of seeing the words one wrote, made public. In any event my teacher did not view this exercise in first-person assertiveness with the same delight that I did, and I had to stay after school to wash the penciled markings from the white paint.

This previously unrecorded event took place in Lucas, Texas, in Collin County, about 8–10 miles east of Allen, east of Highway 75. This is where I was born, in a small house on my grandfather's 168-acre cotton farm. Not much has been written about Lucas. Founded in 1870, Lucas does not even appear on several maps in histories written a century later, nor is there any mention of Lucas in these histories. Lucas was never called a town; it was a "community," indicating something smaller than a town. Communities, it appears, had trouble formally entering into recorded history.

All the history I have of Lucas is from memory, and if I look up the brief entry on Lucas in *The New Handbook of Texas,* the bible of Lone Star fact and lore, it's like looking in a mirror, because I am the author of that memory piece passing as "history." All I know of Lucas comes from personal experience. In the 1940s, the time I defaced public property, Lucas consisted of two stores, three churches (one Baptist, one Methodist, and one First Christian Church), one cotton gin, and one schoolhouse. The schoolhouse was a white wooden building of two stories. On one side of the first story eight grades occupied one half of the building, with a wall separating the youngsters from the ultra-sophisticated high school students on the other side of the first floor. The second floor had a small stage where schoolchildren and adult members of the community put on theatricals and held festive events such as apple bobbing and other party games on Halloween and Christmas. Adjacent to the school was a lighted softball/baseball field. In the summer adult teams played there most nights, and many from the outlying farms came to watch. And there was also a smaller building that was used for women's activities such as quilting. And, rather surprisingly it seems in retrospect, there was also a professional-grade croquet court. The popularity of croquet may well be a forgotten aspect of community life in that Texas of long ago. The *WPA Guide to Texas,* published in 1940, mentions "roque" courts in McAllen, Texas, in the Valley. Incidentally there is no mention of Lucas in the *WPA Guide.* Nor is there any mention of Lucas in the 1939–1940 edition of *The Texas Almanac,* that annual and usually dependable complication of fact and reality. Princeton, Prosper, Frisco, and Josephine, the latter a place I have never heard of, are all there, but not Lucas. In fact, Lucas does not enter *The Texas Almanac* until 1990–91, under the heading "Lucas, city of." Its population: 2,142. And Josephine? A paltry 508.

We lived in an invisible, unsung place, Lucas, Texas, in the 1940s.

The main business of Lucas and surrounds was raising cotton, the old staple of Southern economy. The land was part of a vast blackland prairie, though I don't think I ever heard the word *prairie* used to describe Collin County when I was growing up. Cotton culture involved a lot of stoop labor, followed by lulls and long hot days of those endless Texas summers, and then, at cotton-picking time, great excitement and anxiety. A prolonged rain could destroy a year's work, just as the absence of rain could do the same, and the vagaries of market conditions were always a worry. Wars, incidentally, were excellent stimulants for higher profits. Armies needed cotton for everything—ammunition, uniforms, and medical supplies.

One year I recall, when the cotton was all picked and packed loosely into a trailer pulled by a tractor, I was placed on the top of the heap by my father and rode high up there, regally, king of the cotton, to the gin, which was less than a mile away. The gin was a strange and somewhat uncomfortable place. My father worked there from time to time, moving the huge bales around with a dolly as though they were feather pillows. There was a scary pond next to the gin, scary because it was filled with water moccasins. And the old men who lolled around the gin, they were scary, too. They would always embarrass me by asking if I slumbered in bed. I would turn red and stammer out a *no,* followed by much laughter.

The culture was entirely Southern. The men dressed in overalls or khaki pants and shirts, and if anybody had walked around in a pair of cowboy boots he would have been laughed out of the county for putting on airs, for being a drugstore cowboy. There were more mules in the county than horses. (Indeed, I discovered long years later in *The Texas Almanac 1939–1940* that Collin County was "one of the leading mule counties in Texas." How about that!)

The significance of the mule in my father's life was made clear to me once when he told about the first John Deere tractor he ever owned. He bought it a few years before I was born. Curious about it—this was later, when I had begun to develop an interest in history—I asked him how he acquired that tractor. (We had the tractor the whole time I was a child. At age five my job was to drive it, very slowly, down the rows of our corn field while my parents, walking behind, pulled and tossed the ripened ears of corn into a trailer.) He said he traded for it. I said traded what? He said he traded his two mules, Tojo and Stud. (The names are interesting. Tojo has its historical resonance, and Stud shows a taste for irony.) I asked where he'd traded the mules and he said he went to the John Deere dealership and traded the mules directly to the dealer.

One of the best things about living on a farm was the food. We had a small truck garden and there were always, in season, plenty of fresh vegetables. Local corn was delicious too. We drank well water out of a tin dipper—delicious. But the really big gastronomical event of the year came at hog-killing time. Every fall when the weather finally turned cold enough, my father and other family members and neighbors would kill a hog and butcher it. They filled a big vat with boiling water and plunged the carcass into it to burn the bristles off. They made use of the whole hog. They made soap from the rendered lard, and they hung hams and bacon in the smokehouse. One year, I must have been five or six, I had a culinary epiphany when I realized that the fresh pork and the red-eyed gravy made from it were about the best things God ever put on this earth for a boy to eat. Of course as a boy all I did was watch the process; I didn't have to do any of the very intensive labor required to bring the pig to the plate. And the biscuits; I almost forgot the biscuits. The biscuits were homemade, too, and delicious. Everything was homemade. Later, when canned biscuits came on the market, my mother was ecstatic, but my father always regarded canned biscuits as a leading indicator of the decline and fall of Western Civilization.

Another favorite from those days was chickens. Everybody raised chickens, and nobody called them free-range either. Fried chicken was an absolute treat, though here too the process of turning a bird into a Sunday dinner was ghastly. It was grandmothers, incidentally, who specialized in killing the chickens. The grandmothers had seen everything, and the murder and dismemberment of one more chicken meant nothing to them. I would try to be somewhere else when the mayhem took place, but I was always right there, front and center, when the fried chicken was being passed around. Chickens were smaller in those days and fed on whatever was at hand and they were incredibly flavorful. The last good chicken was probably consumed in the 1960s. Since then, it's all been downhill: chemicals and bigness and blandness. You'd probably have to go to some third-world country today to find a decent chicken.

Crawfish, which we called crawdads, were another favorite childhood delicacy. There was a tiny stream of running water in the field behind our barn, and in that stream—it wasn't big enough to be called a creek. It wasn't called anything that I can remember; it wasn't an arroyo, we didn't have fancy words like that, it was more like a muddy little ditch—in any event, in that sluggish little ditch of water thrived many crawfish, and I became adept at catching them, using bacon or bread or just about anything for bait. One of the tragic days of my childhood occurred after I had made a big catch. I worked for hours on the steps of the back porch cutting off the tails and putting them in a bowl of water. From here they would be taken into the kitchen and through the alchemy of cooking emerge as fried crawfish tails. But on this day I left the bowl of clean crawfish tails unattended—for only moments, as I went somewhere else in the yard for something, distracted or intrigued by something—only to return, just seconds later, to find that the chickens had gobbled up every single morsel of crawdad tails. Thereafter I didn't care what my grandmothers did to the chickens.

To return to school days, I attended the Lucas School for three years before we moved to McKinney, where my father could find more congenial work than being, in essence, a share-cropper. The Lucas School, in retrospect, did an excellent job of educating its pupils. In my case I learned, as I have said, to read and write; I learned a good deal about the structural rules of grammar; in short, the essential tools that would carry me through the rest of my public school, collegiate, and professional life. Here tribute must be paid to our teacher, the woman who managed to handle eight grades in one room. I remember her name to this day: Inez Smithey. In fact she and her husband Boyd Smithey rented a portion of the house we lived in, my grandfather's house, just down the road from the school, though I can assure you that this proximity earned me no special favors. That house is long gone, the site occupied now by a Methodist church. My mother, I'm fairly certain, would prefer it to have been a Baptist church.

I am unable to recall many details from our classroom experience, though I remember that Mrs. Smithey would spend an hour with one row, while the other rows were set to silent tasks such as reading or practicing penmanship. As a teacher myself, I can't imagine handling the discipline and assignments for eight grades in one room. Of course she didn't have to deal with problems of the kind that teachers face today. Recently, for example, at a school in Manor, near Austin, fights broke out among students, and the police had to come in and arrest several students and haul them off to juvenile delinquency court. It turns out that the warring students were members of two gangs made up of girls: one gang was named *Bad Bitches* and the other was named *Kill a Bitch*. Compared to that, the school at Lucas was a virtual Garden of Eden.

My fascination with words and language began at the Lucas School. One day, for example, we were studying local flora and fauna and the name for a local tree surfaced and somebody, it might well have been me, was at the blackboard and spelled out the word "bo dark." Bo dark, that was a tree we all knew. But then the teacher went to the board and spelled it correctly: bois d'arc. I couldn't believe it. That was another major childhood epiphany. That a tree so common could have such an exotic name—from the French, no less, *c'est incroyable*—and after that the magic and mystery of language were one of the pleasures of my learning experience.

My mother read to me some children's stories, but they did not stick, and I find that my knowledge of children's literature is very sparse and my interest in the genre entirely negligible. Of much more import, as imaginative sources for future writing and thinking, were the countless Westerns on display at the movie houses in the county seat of McKinney, northwest of Lucas, and Plano, to the south. At that time, in the late 1940s, McKinney had three theaters. All the big Westerns—*Red River, Broken Arrow, Winchester 73*—played at the Ritz. They were family films and families saw them. The Texan, located off the square where the Courthouse with its segregated drinking fountains enforced the de facto Jim Crow law of the land, ran Westerns for children mainly. These included the endless array of Republic products and all the films of Gene Autry, Roy Rogers, Johnny Mack Brown, and Lash Larue, along with serials, and some now largely forgotten "Eastern" Westerns, as I think of them today, films based on the novels of James Fenimore Cooper and starring George Montgomery as Hawkeye. These were moccasin and canoe Westerns, and I loved them; they seemed so exotic. In Collin County there were no rivers to speak of and no lakes.

Many of the Western Westerns were ostensibly set in Texas, and from my blackland prairie cotton-field perspective, they dramatized a vision of Texas that set one's pulse a-throbbing. It was the same Texas that I glimpsed later in the novels of Zane Grey. In both, the West was a far more romantic and exciting place than where I lived. Both film and fiction told me that the West, Texas included, was an expanse of vast, endless vistas of desert and prairie populated by cattle and cowboys and desperadoes of nasty mien and short life span. Some of the cowboys were excellent singers and everything always worked out for the best. There were Indians all over the lot, and although some of them were noble, most weren't, and in any event they had as transitory a shelf life as the desperadoes. They died on-screen before we had a chance to see them as anything other than "Other."

Texas, I was made to understand, consisted of men on horseback performing heroic deeds in sun-drenched deserts dotted with saguaro cactus, doubtless imported from Arizona, outside towns named Abilene and Amarillo and Galveston that were surrounded, always, by gorgeous, snow-capped mountains. It was an irresistible dreamscape. The lesson I took away with me, the imprint, was that where I lived, in Southern-striated Texas, with its cotton fields, mules, stoop labor, overalls, and so on, did not really count. What counted was West Texas, out where the deer and the antelope played, and where never was heard a discouraging word. There must have been some pretty discouraging words heard in Collin County kitchens in those days as families left the farms and moved to towns like McKinney where there were better economic prospects. Children never know that they are part of an historical process, but what in fact was happening in my childhood is that the small family farm was receding into history, and post–World War II Texas was entering a period of urbanization that was the wave of the future. In 1940, 60 percent of Texans lived in the country; in 1960, 60 percent lived in cities. Today the figure is roughly 82 percent in cities, 18 percent in rural areas.

Moving to McKinney put me in easy walking distance of those theaters where the Westerns rolled on. And it took me out of cotton fields forever, I thought. But then a few years later we moved closer to Dallas, to Carrollton, at that time a small outlying town, and suddenly, that first summer, needing a job, I found myself, at my dad's behest, hired to chop cotton on a nearby farm (doubtless the site of a mall now). We started at early light, and by noon I was done. I had one of those cotton-field conversions that marked, I would later realize, the lives of three famous Texas writers: Walter P. Webb, Roy Bedichek, and J. Frank Dobie. All three experienced crucial moments in cotton fields when they vowed that whatever else might happen in their lives, they planned to have nothing more to do with cotton. In my own case I got a job caddying at a newly built country club, where work was play, and I hit my first golf ball and observed the indolent lives of very rich young girls at the club swimming pool, and I was pretty much ruined for life.

From a very early age I began reading books in earnest, entire books, or from front to back as people in my part of Texas who read few books were wont to say. One motive, I'm certain, was escape. The other was an incipient interest in language, in how sentences and paragraphs and narrative were constructed for one's pleasure and edification. Novels transported me to places I'd never seen, to worlds beyond those of living on a farm. One of the authors that I favored was Zane Grey. It may be because his books were so omnipresent. Every issue of the Sunday supplement in the *Dallas Morning News* bore on its back cover an ad depicting handsome "leather"-bound sets of Zane Grey's Western novels. The plan was to buy two at the outset and as the months passed, another volume would arrive. Although my family never signed on to this wonderful deal, these books were widely available, and various of them fell into my hands. People who owned copies seemed glad to loan them to somebody interested enough to read them from cover to cover. The school library—this was later, in Carrollton, just north of Dallas—had a set of those "leather"-bound Greys. There was no library, school or otherwise, in my early childhood.

And so it was that in my pre- and teen years, I began to learn about the West from reading, having previously learned about it from the movies. When I left a movie house or finished an exciting Zane Grey novel, I looked around me and saw only the flat blackland prairie of Collin County where romantic Western scenery was in meager supply. The Texas I inhabited was scarcely distinguishable from the rest of Dixie.

Reading in general became a steady form of escape for me, and reading Zane Grey was especially thrilling because Grey's America offered an alternative vision for a Southerner. Like historian Frederick Jackson Turner, President Theodore Roosevelt, novelist Owen Wister, and artist Frederic Remington—all important shapers of the West in the American imagination—Grey turned the West into myth and set up Western U.S. space as a regenerative zone to offset the degeneration and despair of modernism, of urban America, and yes, of the South as well. That's what I say now. As a naïve reader, the very heart and marrow of Grey's massive audience, I don't know how much I thought was myth and how much was living, breathing reality.

From my perspective, Grey's West lay farther on, in Arizona and southern Utah mostly, the West of the Apache and the Navajo and, strangest of all, of the Mormons, a people I absolutely did not get. But there were a few novels set in Texas and I read them as I read the ones set elsewhere. Looking back now from the advanced perspective of Google-assisted research, I can tell you that of his fifty-five Western novels, seven of them have Texas settings. And that there is a book titled *Zane Grey's Arizona* but not one on Zane Grey's Texas. It would be a pretty short book, if there were one.

Grey traveled far and wide in his lifetime. Born in 1872 and bearing the feminine moniker of Pearl Zane Gray (he later dropped Pearl and changed the spelling of Gray), he hailed from Zanesville, Ohio, attended the University of Pennsylvania (another place I know well), pitched for the University nine, became a dentist, and then went into the line of work he was born for, writing romances and ultimately Western romances with irresistible titles like *Last of the Plainsmen, Call of the Canyon,* and *Wanderer of the Wasteland.* He lived for a long time at Lackawaxen, Pennsylvania, and eventually moved to southern California. He visited Arizona numerous times to soak up local landscape color for his novels, and in his capacity as a world-class fisherman he traveled extensively in the South Seas and caught a world-record tiger shark (1,036 pounds) during a visit to Australia. (In his career Grey held twelve world fishing records.) He was also a world-class sexual rogue, as recent biographies have shown. Grey specialized in seducing young women and tormented his long-suffering wife with his serial infidelities. These extramarital adventures perhaps account for all of the passionate clinches and overheated flights of erotic rhetoric in Grey's fictional world. Every gunfighter is a stud, every young female is a peach, even if she doesn't know it.

Grey's travels apparently did not include any extensive trips to Texas. The only time that he visited the state, it appears from the record, is a train layover in El Paso for a few hours, in 1913, during which time he interviewed Texas Ranger Captain John Hughes. Grey was gathering background for his first Texas-based novel, *The Lone Star Ranger,* published in 1915. Grey also drew upon his reading, especially accounts of famed Ranger Leander McNelly, whose operations against Mexican bandits in South Texas during 1875–1876 still stir the imaginations of historians and novelists.

Easily the most interesting of Grey's Texas-based books, in my view, is *West of the Pecos.* Published in 1937, it falls within what one critic calls the third phase of his career, a period of decline from 1926 to 1939, the year of his death.

I am going to have to imagine, because I can't remember, that I read *West of the Pecos* when I was a boy. If I did not, I should have, because the schematic mythology of this novel matches perfectly with the real and the imaginative Texas I have de-

scribed above. The narrative begins in 1865, in a Southern setting redolent of *Gone with the Wind*, published the year before Grey's novel. Templeton Lambeth, lately promoted to the
rank of Colonel, returns to his plantation in Louisiana following the close of the Civil War. Lambeth is tired of raising cotton on poor land and tired of the "ups and downs of a planter's
life." He wants to start over in Texas, where people "are lured
on by something magnetic and compelling." He frees his slaves,
and when his daughter Terrell wanders among the plantation
grounds to say a last goodbye, she notes that "the happy, dancing, singing slaves were gone, and their whitewashed homes
were falling to ruin." One slave, however, is so loyal and so "stal-
wart" and "sober" that he wants to remain in Lambeth's service.
His name is Sambo, and in a bit of a twist, Sambo is actually
from Texas, having been raised on the plains of Texas and sold
to the Lambeth plantation. As a result of his early days in Texas,
Sambo is "one of the few really good negro vaqueros." Thus in
the first three pages a discourse of South vs. West, Louisiana vs.
Texas, and planter vs. cowboy is established. Grey, incidentally,
was ahead of most cowboy romancers in inserting black cowboys into his stories of Western life.

Grey's geography is fuzzy in these opening chapters, perhaps
deliberately so. In Chapter 2 we learn that for most of his life
Lambeth "had lived in that small part of Texas which adjoined
Louisiana." Before this, we had been told that his plantation was
in Louisiana, his brother's in Texas. In any event he wants to find
"the real Texas—the Texas that had fallen at the Alamo and that
in the end had conquered Santa Ana [*sic*], and was now reaching
north and west, an empire in the making." So he and his daughter Terrill and Sambo and his "missus" take to the road. They
spend a night in the capital city, but the girl Terrill "does not
like" Austin. San Antonio is where real Texas begins. The word
"picturesque" proves handy to Grey in describing the colors and
smells of the old mission city, but it is at the Alamo where the
meaning of Texas is spelled out. Lambeth tells his daughter, "We
Southerners lost the Civil War, but we can never lose the glory
of freein' Texas from Spanish rule." Although his history is a

little shaky here, the message is the upbeat one relayed throughout the novel: The West is the place of regeneration, the South is
the site of defeat and despair. East Texas was the South . . . ergo.
So it was that in my high school days in the mid-1950s we made
a pilgrimage to the Alamo, having had no history of our own
worth contemplating in North Texas farming country or in the
soon-to-be-suburbs of Dallas. This was before November 22,
remember. So it was that my family made a trip to and through
mythic Texas and went all the way to Corpus Christi and across
to the Valley and on the way passed by King Ranch, which was
ur-Texas and ours was not even close.

In another formulation of considerable interest, Grey
describes Texas as a "world in itself," a phrase he had first used
back in 1915, in *The Lone Star Ranger*. He may well have originated
this useful concept. Once the Lambeths are on the Western
plains, Sambo theorizes along the same lines: "But Texas done be
as big as de whole Yankeeland." This view of Texas as a unique
space, based on its history as a republic and its status as the biggest state in the Union, is echoed throughout modern Texas self-
puffery, in books and in advertising. George Sessions Perry titled
his breezy 1942 history of the state *Texas: A World in Itself;* John
Bainbridge called his 1961 take on Texas *The Super-Americans;* and
ad campaigns for trucks and beer routinely speak in similarly
grandiose, exceptionalist terms: "A Whole Other Country,"
"The National Beer of Texas."

Once Lambeth's entourage leaves San Antonio, headed west,
iconic Western events come on stage as regularly as they did in
the Cavalcade of Texas, an historical pageant of Texas history
that defined for many the essence of the Texas Centennial, held
at the State Fair Grounds in 1936. (In fact, it's entirely conceiv-
able that Grey turned to Texas for this novel as a result of all the
national publicity the state received in the run-up to and especially during that year that marked the Alamo's centennial as
well as Texas's.) We witness, for example, a buffalo stampede,
see longhorns being trailed to New Mexico, thrill at stirring
accounts of fights with Indians, who are invariably described as
"wild savages" or "red devils," bite our nails at tense confronta-

tions between a hard-case cowboy named Pecos Smith and various ruffians; in short, it's just one damned Western thing after
another. And always those traveling West with the right mo-
tives (Lambeth and his entourage) are empowered by their contact with the raw vitality and energy of trying to wrest a living
from the struggle with nature, redskins, "greasers," and border
riff-raff.

Reading Grey today, I don't find much of interest in the
mechanics of plot and action. And the dialogue is often laugh-
able. Texans in this novel, one and all, say "aboot" instead of
"about." They sound like Canadians. The only time in my experience a Texan says "aboot" is when he's talking about footwear:
a boot. And Grey's black dialect is especially embarrassing.

I have deliberately put off talking about the female lead in
West of the Pecos. Terrill, named after her uncle, who was killed in
the War, is her daddy Lambeth's pride and joy — *except* that she is
not a male. So Daddy makes her dress like a male, and for much
of the novel Terrill masquerades as a boy. It's sort of like Shakespeare, only bad, really bad. Shakespeare. The devoted ex-slave
Sambo has to be dressed down once, as it were, for not taking
her seriously as a "he." Here is what "Missy Till" tells him: "Nig-
ger, never you Missy Till me again; I'm a man!" I have no idea
what I made of this when I was going through puberty and reading Grey. I still don't.

Well, things work out in the end, and Pecos Smith's man-
hood, evident in every hyper-paragraph of description (that "big
gun" on his leg, for example), has its ameliorative effect upon
the cross-dressing Terrill, who learns to deal with the emotions
and stuff that makes her go all soft and mushy at times, very un-
manly, that, and eventually, inevitably, she is won over by the big
stiff. None other than Judge Roy Bean it is who marries them.
Before that, Sambo, likewise reinvigorated by life west of the
Pecos, is the father of twins — "two mo' black cowhands." Pecos
Smith himself has moved beyond a shady past and some close
brushes with the law, to become, at last, a "Texan . . . one of
the moving atoms of the great empire he envisioned." See how
healthy Texas west of the Pecos is! See how it cures the ener-

vating demoralization of decadent cotton culture and miscon-
strued gender identity; it provides a new space for imagining the
American dream of empire.

From his vantage point in California, Zane Grey watched the
West that he loved, the wild spaces of Arizona, etc., gradually
yield to changes wrought by the encroachments of "civilization."
For Grey, as for many Western writers, the West was always
changing, always being lost. The Dude-ification of the West cur-
rently going on in once-remote places like Marfa, west of the
Pecos, would doubtless have made Grey hanker for unspoiled
country farther on, somewhere west of that fabled river, in one
of those magic valleys that define his West, where everything is
static, an Eden without change, where Pecos Smith and his girl-
ish young bride can flourish and propagate in the Texas that Grey
imagined.

Looking at Lucas today, or recently, when I drove up there
for the first time in twenty years, I was struck by the changes —
who would not be? That rich blackland prairie has now become
rich real estate, and Dallas, rather than waiting for everybody in
Collin County to move there, has in fact, in a sense, moved to
Collin County. Or at least that's how it appears to my untrained
social science eye.

In the late 1980s, on a short flight from Lisbon to London,
a woman sitting next to me struck up a conversation. When she
asked me where I was from, I said Texas, and she was excited.
She was dying to see Southfork, she said; it was the one place in
America that she would most like to visit. I told her how much
I wanted to visit her native country, India, but she brushed that
aside and went on with her enthusiasm about Southfork. When
I mentioned that Southfork was in the same county where
I had grown up, she was beside herself, she wanted to know
all about the Ewing ranch. When I told her the whole Southfork thing was a myth, she didn't believe me. Finally I told her
what she wanted to hear: that indeed my family owned a ranch
and that we had made obscene amounts of money from the oil
wells on our expansive prairies. She was happy then, and by that
time we were landing at Heathrow and she could tell her family

and friends that she had met a real Texan, a person of property, drawl, and sprawl.

The TV show *Dallas* westernized us all, and now Collin County has a mythology it can embrace: oil, cattle, big money— none of which reflect the real history of the county. The 2009– 2010 edition of *The Texas Almanac,* under the heading of Lucas— Agriculture, lists these entities: landscape nurseries, corn, wheat, cattle. Thus the erasure continues. The only remnant of the by- gone days of cotton culture is that stadium in Dallas that they didn't name the Cattle Bowl or the Oil Bowl; they named it the Cotton Bowl!

2009

OWENS COUNTRY

The year 2005 marked the centennial of Texas author William A. Owens (1905–1990), and in his home country, northeast Texas, they remembered. That fall, Texas A&M University–Commerce and Paris Junior College hosted a conference bringing together family, friends, scholars, and the general public to celebrate the life and work of the man from Pin Hook. Owens's early life was set in cotton farming culture, on blackland prairie, where the crops were best, or on sandy land, where they were not.

But Owens is important not because of where he grew up but because of the writing he forged out of that time and place. In all, he penned four volumes of autobiographical accounts of his long, arduous path from cotton fields to centers of learning. The first is the best, *This Stubborn Soil*. The title is so evocative that Bert Almon, in a very fine study of Texas memoirs, adapted the title thus: *This Stubborn Self: Texas Autobiographies* (2002). There was hardly any self more stubborn than that of Owens; he had to be stubborn just to survive in that country, pursuing, as he did, decade after decade, the goal of achieving an education.

What Owens set out to do in *This Stubborn Soil* was to create a world already disappearing, in 1966, when the book was published. (He had actually finished the book in 1947, but his agent told him to wait until he was "bigger," i.e., better known as a writer, before telling his own story. Would that many confessional memoirists of our own time had followed this admonition.) The time is pre–World War I America and on into the 1930s.

As a writer Owens faced the same set of problems that nineteenth-century American authors like Hawthorne (and later Henry James) confronted. In a famous passage from James's book on Hawthorne, James described everything that the American writer did not have in contrast with what an older culture— namely, England—already possessed. Wrote James:

> No State, in the European sense of the word, and indeed barely a specific national name. No sovereign, no court, no personal loyalty; no aristocracy, no church, no clergy, no army, no diplomatic service, no gentlemen, no palaces, no castles, nor manors, nor old country houses, no parsonages, nor thatched cottages, nor ivied ruins, no great Universities nor public schools—no Oxford, nor Eton, nor Harrow; no literature, no novels, no museums, no pictures, no political society, no sporting class—no Epson, no Ascot!

This is quite a list. But Pin Hook, Texas, during Owens's youth, made Hawthorne's New England look like a center of high culture. From James's list, Pin Hook had precious little. It had a school and a church, but not quite in the sense that James meant. The school ran for five months a year, squeezed in between seasons of agricultural harvests and plantings, and what it offered for the most part was functional literacy. The church—most assuredly Protestant, in Owens's case Baptist—offered a sense of sin, a hope of salvation in the next life, and, through music, almost in spite of Baptist doctrine, a taste of aesthetic pleasure.

In James's words Hawthorne lived in a "crude and simple society." Such adjectives apply to Pin Hook in spades. Hawthorne solved his artistic problem in part by turning to the Puritan past for the stuff of romance, or else turning inward to explore the human psyche. Owens, who faced a much thinner society and therefore a more difficult literary problem, chose another tradition than romance—that of realism—and in his books he hewed to the gritty facts of his agrarian roots. The opening paragraph of *This Stubborn Soil* masterfully situates the writer in relation to the literary problem at hand:

> If one was born in Paris or London or New York, or even in Dallas, to name a place closer to home, he has, when writing about himself, only to mention the city and the reader pictures place, buildings, people and he can go ahead to particulars about himself and his family. But since I was born in Pin Hook, Texas, a place whose character has not been made known to the world generally, I must begin by writing all I know or ever heard about it.

For anyone interested in visiting Pin Hook today, it is about a half-hour's drive north of Paris and just five miles from the Red River. All that remains of Pin Hook—there was never much there—is a graveyard.

In thinking about Owens's accomplishment, it is helpful to speculate about such precedents as might have shaped his intentions, or provided models by which he could explore the blank history of a place unknown to the world. According to Owens, one such model was W. H. Hudson, famous for his romance *Green Mansions,* but important to Owens for his autobiographies *Far Away and Long Ago* and *The Purple Land.* On the advice of his freshman English teacher at Paris Junior College, Owens read Hudson's books, presumably long before he had any intentions of writing about Pin Hook. Like Owens, Hudson lived in a frontier society—the Argentine pampas—where nature could be confronted directly. Like Owens, he experienced setbacks from his family's economic reverses. Like Owens, he felt the allure of cities and sought wider worlds. But there are also many substantial differences between the frontier available to Hudson and that available to Owens. Hudson's was exotic, Owens's prosaic;

Hudson's filled with adventures, Owens's filled with grinding labor. There was also a major difference in the cities available to each youth. For Owens there was Paris, a county seat, and Dallas. Paris could offer excitement only to a country youth who had literally never been anywhere; Dallas offered little more than a kind of Dreiserian bleakness. Hudson's city, on the other hand, was Buenos Aires, a metropolis of almost Biblical extremes. It was, for example, possibly the most pestilential city in the world at that time. For literary possibilities, Buenos Aires offered incredible, Dantean scenes of human suffering and misery. One sticks in my mind: a place where animals were slaughtered, a place of blood, offal, and a stench of hellish intensity. Everything in Owens's world was cut to a smaller, less colorful pattern. What I am suggesting is that there are frontiers and frontiers, and Owens inherited one in black and white, not Cinemascope.

The subtitle of Owens's book, "A Frontier Boyhood," is a significant designation in light of the fact that Frederick Jackson Turner, in 1893, had declared the frontier over (based on the census of 1890), but Owens, looking back on his childhood, knew it wasn't over in northeast Texas where he lived, not by a long shot. And this was not the frontier we normally think of; it was not a romantic site of open range or unexplored, unsettled territory. Owens's frontier was that of small tenancy cotton farms, an agrarian zone of hard times mixed with sporadic religious fervor and, in Owens's case, a dogged determination to acquire an education against all odds. Before he started school, weather and dirt defined his existence. Owens is very good on dirt: "My toys were the dirt, and a stick to dig the dirt. No one could live closer to the earth than I did. I dug the sand, I rolled in it, I covered myself with it. Before my first year had passed I had eaten the peck of dirt everyone, Pin Hook people said, is entitled to. I had learned the feel, the smell, the taste of earth."

It is hard to exaggerate the provinciality of Owens's northeast Texas upbringing. At one point he and his brother Dewey are taking a wagonload of peanuts to Paris to sell when they come upon a scene that is wholly unfamiliar to the narrator:

On one side of a fence the grass was dry and brown, on the other, watered and green. On the green side there were big shade trees and sprays of water turning slowly in the sun. It was the prettiest pasture I had ever seen. Men were walking in it, but I could not tell what they were doing.

"What's that?" I asked Dewey.

"Golf course. They're playing golf."

This was something new to me, a game that took enough room to make a cow pasture. It took us a long time to go past, and I watched and asked questions. Dewey had seen it before but only from the road. I watched the men but could not tell what they were doing. From what I could see, I thought they might as well be working.

"Town folks," Dewey said. "They don't know much about working."

Another possible influence upon Owens's conception of autobiography was, I believe, John Bunyan. *This Stubborn Soil* opens with a humorous epigraph from Bunyan—"Some said, John, print it; others said, Not so; Some said, It might be good; others said, No"—and it is tempting to see *This Stubborn Soil* and especially the second volume, *A Season of Weathering,* as spiritual autobiography. Only in Owens's case spiritual has to be redefined away from a religious context to something like the human spirit or the humanistic imagination. Both books dramatize—and do not preach about—the struggle to achieve an education, a liberated mind. In *A Season of Weathering* the young hero, having made a commitment to live in town in order to escape the common fate of Pin Hook—unrelenting toil in a climate of ignorance and prejudice—is faced with three choices: (1) further education in order to become a country school teacher, (2) renunciation of secular knowledge and concentration on one book, the Bible, in order to become a minister (this, incidentally, was the shortest route to virtue; it only took about twenty minutes to declare oneself a preacher and set up shop), and (3) apprenticeship to a

Dale Carnegie–like self-help program of discipline, work, and devotion to S. H. Kress five-and-dime stores in order to become a success in business. Owens's pilgrim chooses country school teaching, only to be forced to abandon his career to seek once and for all his destiny in the city. The book closes with the hero's eyes set on Dallas.

There is today a great, yawning gulf between the urban experience of many Texans and the rural experience of writers like William A. Owens. The cotton side of the Texas experience is fading, fading. Dobie, Bedichek, and Webb each had something to do with that, incidentally. Here is Webb on farming (he means cotton farming): "I never appreciated the nobility of farming. All I ever got out of it was sore fingers." And here is Bedichek: "So I quit right in the middle of a row, chopping cotton." Bedichek walked out of that cotton field and moved to Austin to attend the university. Dobie himself, despite his ranching background, had one experience with growing cotton, and that was enough. In one of his essays he recalls, "All ranch work was congenial to me as I grew up, even doctoring wormy calves by day and skinning dead ones by lantern light, but the year we boys tried raising a bale of cotton remains a dark blot." Cotton fields, I suspect, made many a boy yearn for bright lights and university towers.

The fact is, Dobie and Webb (and to a lesser extent Bedichek) had scant interest in what happened east of IH-35. All they cared about was cows, drought, sagebrush, barbed wire, coyotes, windmills, longhorns—a great long list of Western critters and icons. Their imagination, which always stayed west of the Pecos and rarely strayed east of Austin, was scarcely indistinguishable from that of Zane Grey.

Perhaps the final slippage of cotton culture from the consciousness of Texans can be found in Mary Karr's *The Liars' Club*. At one point, Karr writes, her grandmother moved out to West Texas and bought a "cotton ranch." The distinction between farm and ranch is being lost. The word ranch has more prestige, it appears, than the word farm, and hence all farms are ranches. Here's a simple catechism: Farm = cotton; Ranch = cattle.

Three or four years ago, I realized to my dismay that my students had absolutely no knowledge of cotton farming. I could tell from their blank gazes every time I brought up the subject. Then I would forget about this response, or non-response, until the same thing happened the next year. The exact same thing. At a certain point in one's teaching career, everything happens over and over.

So the third or fourth time I saw those same blank looks, I decided to try to give them some idea of what chopping and picking cotton might be like. As it happened, one of my students was going to Rockdale to visit sites featured in George Sessions Perry's *Hold Autumn in Your Hand,* and I asked her to bring back a cotton boll if she could find one (it was September), and she did bring back a nice full boll of fluffy cotton, and I passed it around and tried to describe how long a cotton sack was and how long it took to fill it up (nearly forever, if you were a child). I did the whole cotton thing, and I might as well have been talking about the Punic Wars.

Just as knowledge of the Southern part of Texas history has faded away, so has awareness of the major writers east of IH-35. While one would think Owens's place in Texas letters should be secure, it most assuredly is not. After all, there aren't many books in the same league with *This Stubborn Soil.* John Graves, for example, has called it "one of the best books ever written about our part of the world." Yet Owens belongs to the part of Texas that keeps being forgotten or erased—East Texas. In a recent section on Texas literature published in the *Dallas Morning News* in 2005, the same year as Owens's centennial, a list of the seven most important Texas writers was featured. The list included some obvious and inevitable choices: Katherine Anne Porter, Larry McMurtry, John Graves, and Cormac McCarthy— but it also included Stephen Harrigan, Edwin (Bud) Shrake, and Terry Southern. You will notice that the magnificent seven does not include anybody east of IH-35. No William A. Owens, no William Humphrey, no William Goyen, no George Sessions Perry. Instead, a place is made for Terry Southern, author of the camp porno send-up *Candy;* the screenplay for *Dr. Strange-*

love, which contains only one Texas-based character; a collection of undistinguished short stories set in Texas (*Red-Dirt Marijuana*); and one undistinguished short novel set in Texas (*Texas Summer*). Terry Southern is not a major Texas writer. William A. Owens is. Just for the record, my list would consist of Katherine Anne Porter, Larry McMurtry, John Graves, Cormac McCarthy, J. Frank Dobie, Américo Paredes, and William A. Owens.

The *Morning News* also printed a literary map of the state, but it too ignored all the important East Texas authors, containing no mention of Owens, Humphrey, Goyen, or Perry. The only writer east of the great IH-35 divide singled out for praise was Edward Swift of Splendora, whose novel titled *Splendora* relates the adventures of a man returning to his small-town East Texas roots dressed as a woman. His East Texas is a place where women are women and the men are too.

As we move forward, or is it backward, into the future, Owens's book will become all the more important, and eventually, the way things are going, its language and content will become as remote as Chaucer. Future editions will need careful annotation because nobody will know what the simplest words or phrases mean. Except perhaps in northeast Texas, where people are not as likely to forget what it once meant to chop cotton.

2006

I met Bill Owens in the late 1970s when he came to the University of Texas to teach a summer course in the English department. We had lunch and talked shop. He was always working on two or three projects at once and was a model of what dedication, discipline, and intelligence could accomplish.

From time to time over the years he would blow into town, and I use that word *blow* deliberately. He was always in motion, it seemed to me, and he came in like a spring shower—freshening and invigorating—and what I remember most is that he'd call and say you want to have lunch, and I'd say yes, and directly there'd be another call, moving the time because there was going to be somebody else at lunch, and finally it would be all set and there would be three or four people for lunch; Owens didn't want to waste lunch on one person, he had about five irons in the fire every time I saw him and he wanted that lunch to be productive.

He had a ton of energy, and like a good boxer, he never stopped moving. And he had twinkly eyes, like Santa Claus. He was a very kind man and a very inspiring writer to know.

In 1983 he came to a big conference on Texas writing that was held at the University of Texas and delivered a talk titled "Regionalism and Universality." In it he gave an overview of his career and an assessment of the need to leave one's region in order to apprehend a larger world. He described the limitations of his early views in a manner familiar to most people who grew up in rural Texas: "All that time I was an unreconstructed southerner, as well as a Texas chauvinist of the J. Frank Dobie persuasion, with no waverings at all until I traveled in the world north of the Red River and encountered other ways of thinking." That statement would apply in some part, I think, to every writer discussed in this book.

WHITE LIKE ME

When the Supreme Court handed down its groundbreaking *Brown v. Board of Education* decision fifty years ago, I was working on my curveball and didn't notice. There were other momentous events of 1954, of course—the McCarthy hearings, the first stirring of American interest in Vietnam, the advent of Elvis—but the most important and far-reaching on the home front was the Court's ruling to end the "separate but equal" doctrine. Still, as someone who had grown up in a segregated world, I didn't really understand the emotional and psychological impact of Jim Crow until 1961, when I read a book called *Black Like Me*. Written by John Howard Griffin, it was a remarkable account of a journey through the Deep South by a white man posing as a Negro. Today this American classic is little known among my students at the University of Texas, but a "definitive edition," published in 2004 by San Antonio's Wings Press, is aimed at a whole new generation of readers.

Griffin lived an extraordinary life. Born in Dallas in 1920, he left home at fifteen to travel alone to France, where he pursued—in French—a classical education at the Lycée Descartes in Tours and also studied medicine and music, which had always interested him. With the onset of World War II, he joined the French Resistance, helping transport to safety Jewish children disguised as mental patients. Returning to Dallas in 1941, he joined the Army Air Forces and spent three years in the

South Pacific, studying the indigenous culture of a remote island in the Solomons. It was there, in 1945, that he suffered an injury that would leave him blind for seven years. In 1955 he became paralyzed for a year from a case of spinal malaria contracted during his time in the islands.

By then Griffin was living on a farm near Mansfield, southeast of Fort Worth, and the next year he became involved in efforts to integrate the town's school system. Three years later he embarked upon his next station of the cross: He undertook, as one writer has put it, "the pilgrimage par excellence of our time."

Griffin worked out an arrangement with the black magazine *Sepia,* whose offices were in Fort Worth. In return for funding his trip through the South, he would write up an account to be published in the magazine upon his return. And so, in the fall of 1959, Griffin shaved his head and, under a doctor's supervision, took pills and sun-lamp treatments to darken his skin. When he looked in a mirror, what he saw was shocking: "the face and shoulders of a stranger—a fierce, bald, very dark Negro—glared at me from the glass," he wrote. "He in no way resembled me." He decided to enter the Negro world in New Orleans, a city he knew well, and immediately began to experience the difficulties of ordinary life on the wrong side of the color line. Everything that white people took for granted—finding a place to eat, getting a drink of water, locating a restroom—became a logistical problem. Whites would sell him cigarettes in a drugstore but would not give him a glass of water.

To most whites he was either invisible or despised. The same street barkers who had solicited him to enter their bars when he was a white man ignored him as a black man. A young female clerk in a store who had been friendly to him when he was white now looked at him as if he didn't exist. He was Ralph Ellison's Invisible Man. But among the city's Negroes, he was accepted and given help. One man, Sterling Williams, who operated a shoe-shine stand, was amazed when Griffin told him that he had come there earlier as a white man and had his shoes shined. Williams became an ally and an adviser, and Griffin spent a week shining shoes. He moved on to Mississippi, where the Negro was not a second-class citizen but a "tenth-class citizen." Mississippi was awful, a nightmare. Every Negro man was called a boy, and Griffin was warned by other blacks to not even look at a movie poster of a white woman. The next stop was Mobile, Alabama, then Montgomery, then Atlanta. As a black man hitchhiking in the Deep South, Griffin got many rides from white men, nearly all of whom wanted to talk about Negroes' sexuality. Everywhere he turned, the racial divide was the overriding issue of the day. Toward the end of his two-month journey, as his color faded, he took to "zigzagging," going white by day, black by night.

Once Griffin's *Sepia* pieces began to appear, in March of 1960, he ceased to be a private figure. There were demands for interviews in the press and on TV. In Mansfield, he was met with stony silence and hung in effigy. After he died, in 1980, an urban legend circulated that he had had cancer caused by the skin-darkening treatments. In fact, he died from a combination of longstanding problems stemming from diabetes and a heart condition.

Black Like Me, whose title was taken from a Langston Hughes poem, has sold more than 11 million copies and has been translated into fourteen languages. Reading it became a rite of passage for many Americans who knew that segregation was wrong but did not know what it felt like to be black. Griffin showed us.

Before I read it, my sense of blackness—of Otherness, one might say today—was that of a middle-class Southern white youth. I grew up on a cotton farm in Collin County, and in our family, blacks were referred to as "colored" or "Negroes" but never the other word. I heard the other word on the school grounds, in public places, and from an early age associated it with people who were either ignorant or white trash, depending on the speaker. My mother had somehow not yielded to the easy conformity of white racialist language of the rural culture of the KKK days when she was growing up. All of this was long before the terms "African American" or "black" became standard usage.

The color line was particularly noticeable at the county courthouse in McKinney, where water fountains were designated "For Whites" and "For Colored Only," and I was also aware that Negroes sat somewhere else in the movie theaters where my cousins and I watched Westerns and the Bowery Boys, but the enforced separation of the races seemed as natural as the rules governing Sunday school dress.

In Carrollton, a suburb of Dallas where we moved in the early fifties, I came into contact with more blacks, but not in school. The summer of 1954, my dad got me a job chopping cotton on a nearby farm. I had thought I was done with that kind of labor forever, and indeed I was. I lasted only one day, and the next I went to work as a caddie at a country club that had just opened east of town. The very idea of a country club was exotic in the extreme, and the Columbian Country Club especially so because it was Jewish. The caddies were comprised of white and black boys who wanted to make some money. Carrying one bag for eighteen holes was $3, a double $5. This was good money and it certainly beat picking cotton. The system at the golf course was instructively democratic. Black and white competed equally, and the first to arrive in the morning, long before sunup, received the first assignment. The days were long and hot, and the boys, all thrown together, passed the time talking about everything or hitting golf balls in a nearby field. It was the best job I ever had as a youth. Near the clubhouse, where we were all forbidden to go, was a swimming pool where the daughters of the rich sunbathed or swam in sumptuous idleness. We could look but not touch. It was really a lesson in race, class, and privilege. It was the American dream all down the line—except, of course, for the young black boys, who at day's end returned home to a separate and unequal existence.

The Carrollton schools remained segregated through my four years of high school, 1954 to 1958, yet black culture was making itself felt in all sorts of ways. Gordon McLendon's KLIF-AM played a lot of black dirty-bop songs like "Work with Me Annie" and its sequel "Annie Had a Baby (Can't Work No More)," songs that had a different rhythm and content from those on TV's *Your Hit Parade*. The subversive impact of that music on white teenagers growing up on the radio range can hardly be overstated.

After I graduated, nothing much changed in Carrollton, except that black high school students were bused to Denton, twenty-five miles away. I went off to Texas Christian University, in Fort Worth, where one of the boys in my all-white dorm had 28 pairs of shoes, and I learned something else about the American dream. But it was on a bus that I got my first taste of what it might be like to be black. When I would go back to Carrollton for weekend visits, I always rode a Trailways bus to Dallas and changed buses there. As everybody knows, buses were the main battleground in the early days of integration. I didn't know that in 1958, but on one of those trips, as people were boarding, I was sitting about halfway back when a loud altercation broke out. An elderly white man was shouting at a young black woman who had dared to take a seat in the front. His anger and yelling drove her to the back of the bus. The rest of us sat in silence—embarrassed, I like to think—and I was humiliated by my failure to challenge the old racist. The memory burns in my mind all these years later, and it is the only bus trip I made that year about which I can recall any details at all.

Black Like Me received widespread critical praise when it was published—except in the black community, where commentary was sparse and critical. Malcolm X, for example, dismissed the book in his autobiography: "If it was a frightening experience for him as nothing but a make-believe Negro for 66 days, then you think about what *real* Negroes in America have gone through for 400 years." But there is another side to black responses to Griffin's book. Contemporary African American artist Glenn Ligon uses Griffin's words as the subject of his powerful painting, *Black Like Me #2*. A sentence from the book—"All traces of the Griffin I had been were wiped from existence"—is stenciled into the painting and through repetition and descent into blackness Ligon dramatizes the truth of Griffin's experience.

Black Like Me came along before Selma, before the murder of

Medgar Evers, before Martin Luther King Jr. gave his "I have a dream" speech. It arrived before there was a black canon in colleges and universities. The book had a moral power that has not diminished with time. It still has things to teach us about the past—and the present.

2004

This piece is the kind of thing I very much enjoy doing—revisiting a book years later that had made a strong impression when I read it the first time. The title was a natural.

COTTON TALE

Although cattle, cactus, and cowboys define most people's idea of the major motifs of Texas literature, a fourth *C* belongs at the top of that list: cotton. King Cotton. From the post–Civil War era to the middle of the twentieth century, it was cotton, not cattle, that propelled Texas's agrarian economy. "Cattle ran a distant second to cotton," wrote historian John Spratt in *The Road to Spindletop*. "In dollar value of the product, in number of persons employed, and in industrial activity generated, cotton stood alone—far in advance of all competitors."

Years before such classics of cattle culture as *Red River, Giant,* and *Lonesome Dove* defined the state to the world, a Texas novel that wasn't about cowboys or big ranches or longhorns won critical acclaim: it was about a tenant farmer who worked sixty-eight acres of rich blackland soil in what was unmistakably Milam County, some sixty miles northeast of Austin. The book, George Sessions Perry's *Hold Autumn in Your Hand,* won a Texas Institute of Letters award in 1941 and an American Booksellers Award the next year. (Many accounts state that Perry's novel won a National Book Award, but that is a mistake; that award did not come into being until 1950.) The novel was also made into a celebrated film in 1945 titled *The Southerner,* directed by world-class French auteur Jean Renoir. All of this and no cowboys. Although Perry is not well known now, he cut a wide swath in his day.

Perry never wrote anything as good after *Hold Autumn in Your*

Hand, but in it he created the best picture we have of a vanished way of life—a world of subsistence farming and the yearlong ritual of planting and picking cotton. In another of his books, *Cities of America,* Perry summed up the importance of cotton culture in pre–World War II Texas: "The mainstay of our existence, the thing on which we bet most heavily in labor and the future, was cotton, and the corn needed to empower our mules to cultivate that cotton. In those days, if boll weevils, droughts or floods destroyed the cotton, we, as a community, were destitute." By the time he wrote that, in 1947, the end of the old means of cotton production—by hand, by tenant farmers—was inevitable; by 1950 the cost of producing a bale of cotton the old way was $45, compared with $11 and a few pennies by machine. The era of the cotton picker was doomed as certainly as "the clipper ships, the prairie schooners, and the Mississippi River steamboats," Perry noted in a 1952 article for the *Saturday Evening Post,* "I Hate to See Those Cotton Pickers Go." But go they did, and no amount of Old South nostalgia would bring them back. Nowadays, if you ever hear anybody say, "It's none of their cotton-pickin' business," you know you're listening to the real voice of old-time Texas.

Hold Autumn in Your Hand might be called "Little Farmhouse on the Blackland Prairie." Sam Tucker is a 38-year-old barely literate sharecropper who has been farming "sandy land" (thin, unproductive soil that produces only "nubbins") or, even worse, toiling in a gang of agricultural peons for a big landowner named Ruston. He goes to Ruston and works out a deal to farm a small piece of rich ground that is lying fallow. Sam wants a chance to plumb the mysteries of black "gumbo," the thick, deep blackland soil that produces the best cotton. It is a way for him to prove to himself that he is a real farmer and a good man. A big plus for Sam is that the property is on the San Gabriel River (called the San Pedro in the novel), northwest of Hackberry (Perry's name for his hometown of Rockdale, located at the intersection of U.S. Highway 79, FM 908, and FM 487). When Perry lived in Rockdale, from his birth, in 1910, until the mid-fifties, the town's population hovered around two thousand. It tripled in the early fifties, when Alcoa built a huge plant southwest of town to take advantage of deposits of lignite, a cheap energy source that had been mined at that site since the late nineteenth century. The advent of Alcoa changed everything; in another 1952 *Post* article, Perry dubbed Rockdale "The Town Where It Rains Money." Today the Alcoa plant still hums along and Rockdale's population holds steady at just over five thousand.

A town man, Perry closely observed the rural folk who came to Rockdale on Saturday afternoons, and he also encountered them during the many hours he spent hunting and fishing in the nearby countryside, including the very farm where the novel is set. Out of such knowledge he crafted a book chock-full of colorful rural idioms, scraps of songs, and the mores of a raw-boned American peasantry. Perry's sure-footed sense of the culture rings true throughout. One character is named Clappy Finley because he has a "perennial dose of claps." When Sam takes his cow to be bred with a neighbor's bull under the cover of darkness, he reasons that "it was just like swiping a ride on the train. It's goin where it's goin anyhow." Sam's middle name, White, is the name of the doctor who delivered him and who was never paid for his services.

Once Ruston agrees to Sam's proposition to farm the parcel of land on the San Gabriel, Sam, his wife, Nona, their two kids, Daisy and Jot, and Sam's irascible grandmother move into a shack on the place and begin the yearlong cycle of what Sam thinks of as a "play-pretty year." "Play-pretty" is just one of many phrases in the novel that puzzle the mostly suburban-bred students in my southwestern literature course at UT Austin. The old rural usage refers to a toy, and breaking and farming sixty-eight acres of intractable, sticky black soil is Sam's idea of fun. Every day is like Christmas to Sam Tucker as long as he can be his own boss and grow his crops. Although he has never heard of Thomas Jefferson's writings on political agronomy, he is the embodiment of Jefferson's vision of the yeoman farmer.

The tale takes place in the dead-end days of the Great Depression. Internal evidence, such as references to "back in '36"

and the "Twin Days" (February 28 and 29), points to 1940, a
leap year, as the most probable time frame. In 1940 the Depression was still playing in Milam County, and by then it must
have seemed a permanent road show. Unemployment rates in
many rural counties in Texas that year were still around 20 percent; FDR's vaunted New Deal hadn't done a thing to change that
alarming statistic. The Tuckers are so "pore" they don't have the
money to buy a new skillet, and Nona has to hold hers at just
the right angle to keep the grease from leaking out through a
hole. Their diet is echt Texas poor white Depression fare: "short-
varmints" such as squirrels and opossum and lots of cornbread
and beans. East Texans had been dining on a diet of cornbread,
bacon, and beans since before the Civil War, and they still were.
A pound of coffee is like manna from heaven, a ready-made
cigarette a Midas-like luxury.

The novel begins as an indictment of a punishing economic
system, a theme that was hardly unique at the time; the thirties
had been filled with photojournalism and fiction devoted to the
evils of tenant farming. James Agee's *Let Us Now Praise Famous
Men,* with its memorable photos by Walker Evans, set the standard for documentary realism, just as Steinbeck's *The Grapes of
Wrath* did for fiction. Down in Texas, where cotton was every
bit as royal as it was in the Deep South, authors now long forgotten labored in the fields of fiction—writers like Dorothy
Scarborough (*In the Land of Cotton*), Ruth Cross (*The Golden
Cocoon*), Laura Smith Krey (*And Tell of Time*), and many others.
In *The White Scourge* (1940), Edward Everett Davis, perhaps the
most lurid of the cotton laureates, limned the cotton field as "the
great open air slum of the South, a perennial Hades of poverty,
ignorance, and social depravity." According to Davis, whose cre-
dentials included being the dean of North Texas Agricultural
College (now the University of Texas at Arlington), cotton culture consisted of a bottom-dog mongrel mix of "lowly blacks,
peonized Mexicans, and moronic whites numbering into several millions." Davis's amateurish fiction can still provoke strong
reactions. The title page of one of the copies at the Center for
American History at the University of Texas at Austin carries an

irate reader's penciled note: "Never has there been a 'so called educated man' that is so filled with hate and prejudice!"

The curious thing about Perry's novel, however, is how quickly it abandons its criticism of tenant farming and, instead, becomes a prose paean to the agrarian ideal. A farmer, Perry writes, is "a man who feels out the darkest of mysteries with the tendrils of his imagination." In fertile ground, corn grows "like plants in a myth." The harvest is "the deeply satisfying thing that must come rhythmically at the end of the land cycle." Perry is writing a form of georgic pastoral that goes all the way back to Virgil. The novel is, finally, about the satisfactions of farming the good earth, contrasted with the sterile environment of another kind of labor: working on an assembly line in an automobile plant in Houston.

Throughout the novel, Houston looms as the magnet that inexorably pulls the sons of the soil away from the land and the joys of woods and fields, river and mystery, to the city and its soulless factory jobs, where one is no longer master of his time and labor. Once, before he was married, Sam had worked in a Ford factory in Houston, rubbing fenders with a compound to even out the paint. The job paid well, but there was a cost to the spirit that he could not accept: "The thing was that a man could not have the proper diet rubbing fenders. It took all that stuff out of you and didn't put anything back." Sam remembers this more than once during his play-pretty year, because the truth that he doesn't want to accept is that Houston and another killing factory job are what await him. Perry's original last chapter contained several pages of gloomy prophesy of the inevitable end of Sam's life on the farm. One passage contrasts the beauty and bounty of the river, where Sam fishes and alongside which he hunts, with another, urban "river of steel and banana oil, a river that only took things out of you and gave nothing back except four dollars a day." What Sam fears, in another passage, is "the robot life of an assembly line attendant." But Perry's publisher preferred a more upbeat ending, and these passages— about five pages in all—were deleted.

Even so, the attentive reader finds plenty of hints in the novel to suggest that the siren call of Houston's higher wages is present and potent and in the end will prove irresistible. The reader even begins to understand that Sam's play-pretty year has in some ways been a childish self-indulgence having more to do with his needs than with those of his family, though Sam does all that any man could to keep his family fed and clothed and sheltered in a time when, as FDR famously said, one-third of the nation fell short in each of these requirements for a decent life.

The lovely, poetic title of Perry's novel refers not to cotton but to the produce from a vegetable garden (or what Texans used to call a truck garden). The Tuckers live so far out in the sticks they haven't heard of canning and preserving vegetables, and a crisis is precipitated when the youngest child, Jot, grows ill with "spring sickness," or pellagra, a vitamin deficiency that ravaged poor families in the thirties. Later, his sister, Daisy, who attends school and has listened to the remedy prescribed by the county home-demonstration agent, tells her family of a way to prevent pellagra. The solution is fresh vegetables, and the Tuckers learn that a garden of vegetables, preserved in jars, allows one to realize, as Sam imagines it, "the dream . . . of holding autumn in his hand throughout the winter." Sam's dream is almost destroyed by his bad neighbor, Henry Devers, who, out of envy and pure meanness, lets his animals loose in Sam's garden. Sam wins the day, however, by trading bragging rights on the giant catfish he has caught for the vegetables in Henry's garden.

Although Sam is victorious on that front, his cotton crop is destroyed. Among all the disastrous things that can happen to a cotton crop, the two worst are not enough rain and too much rain at the wrong time. In the novel Sam has wonderful cotton, a bale an acre, until the rains come and the river floods the fields.

The farm that gave Perry the biggest success of his career had a peculiar hold on his imagination. In a book he later wrote about farming (*Tales of a Foolish Farmer*), he spoke of how he "envied Sam Tucker" and wished to "undergo the same rigors." With money from the novel and film, Perry satisfied his "thirst for personal agronomy" by buying the "little *Hold Autumn in Your Hand* farm" as well as a larger farm about a mile away, on Brushy

Creek. But ironically, instead of growing crops, he had the farms converted to grazing land and stocked them with Hereford cattle.

In modern Rockdale Perry's memory is kept green by the Lucy Hill Patterson Memorial Library and in the recollections of the steadily declining number of people who knew Perry personally. The library possesses a number of documents relating to Perry's life and works. There is also a historical marker, installed in 1992. This came about through the efforts of Mark Brady, a dynamic history teacher at Rockdale High, and his students. Within an easy walk of the marker is the house at 339 Green Street, where Perry and his wife, Claire Hodges Perry, lived in the thirties, during the lean years of his apprenticeship to the craft of writing.

Traces of the old agrarian economy are evident everywhere in modern Rockdale. The county fair, held every October, is still a big deal, and the Premium Food Preservation Awards, a competition for home-canned foods, offers ten adult and four youth prizes. When I was there in 1998, the October 8 edition of the weekly *Rockdale Reporter* carried an article on "pig showmanship" written by an extension agent aptly named Joel Pigg. There was also an amazing story in the paper about a local catfish that was found to contain the remains of a baby deer. Such details could easily have appeared in Perry's novel.

The text of the historical marker ends with a phrase that must puzzle some people: "before his death in 1956–57." But in fact the exact date of Perry's death is unknown. A life that had been made increasingly difficult by acute arthritis, depression, and a nervous breakdown had a sad ending. Perry and his wife were living in their vacation home in Guilford, Connecticut, when, on December 13, 1956, he vanished. After two months of extensive search efforts, Perry's body was found, dressed only in socks, in a river about two miles from his home. Not long before his disappearance Perry had told friends, "The best thing I can do in this depressed state is jump into the river and swim to the North Pole or run into the woods until I drop." The discovery of his body made the front page of the *Dallas Morning News*.

One day that October of 1998, Bill Cooke, the owner of the *Rockdale Reporter,* and I spent part of a sunny afternoon searching for the *Hold Autumn* farm. Leaving Rockdale on FM 908, at the north edge of town, we drove past the cemetery where Perry and his wife are buried. Continuing on for about five and a half miles, through a picturesque countryside marked by clumps of post oak and fields where fat cattle grazed, we crossed an un-marked bridge over Brushy Creek, then kept going for two and a half miles until we got to the place where County Road 432, a gravel road, runs into FM 908 from the left. The parcel of land just off FM 908 to the right was covered with grass and bor-dered on the north side by a line of dense brush and tall trees that conceal the San Gabriel River as it winds its way eastward. The mighty San Gabriel, which once flooded thousands of acres from the *Hold Autumn* farm to the east, is now much diminished by upstream dams.

As near as we could tell, Sam Tucker's and Perry's little farm was just here, between the river and the road. But like Perry, you have to use your imagination to conjure the way it was in his novel.

1999

CATCHER IN THE RAW

Larry McMurtry's first novel, *Horseman, Pass By* has been almost continuously in print in paperback editions since its publication in 1961. Helped along by *Hud,* the popular and critically acclaimed 1963 film adaptation, it remains a mainstay of courses like Life and Literature of the Southwest. Short, thematically rich, and tailor-made for the classroom, *Horseman, Pass By* rolls on. I teach it every semester in my sw Life and Lit course at the University of Texas at Austin. Over the years student responses to the novel have always been a barometer of the zeitgeist. In the early 1990s when Political Correctness struck the campus like a virulent infection, my P.C. students were appalled at the racism and sexism of the culture described in the novel. A few years later they focused on the threat of hoof-and-mouth disease (this was during the Mad Cow scare), and their vegetarian minds were much agitated. Then for a few years they were concerned about another cow-related issue: bestiality. Today they struggle to understand the difference between a ranch and a farm.

J. Frank Dobie, McMurtry's most famous predecessor, read *Horseman, Pass By* in galleys but did not salute it. Although Dobie liked its depiction of the old cattleman and its bias in favor of ranching as opposed to oil, the book was far too sexually explicit for him to be entirely comfortable with it. Sex might be acceptable in D. H. Lawrence (Dobie owned numerous editions of *Lady Chatterley's Lover*), but it was not to be brooked in Texas literature. Dobie's generation hailed from the Victorian era, and they were a tad squeamish about the rowdy vernacular—in print, that is. In private, around a campfire, Dobie, Webb, and Bedichek loved dirty jokes, and Dobie, late in life, collected materials for a book to be titled "Piss and Vinegar." Bedichek wrote some raunchy and very funny letters. But in their published works sex plays no part; Dobie's cowboys were sexless as newts.

Academics were alarmed at McMurtry's novel as well. A well-known scholar of southwestern lit at TCU, the late Mabel Major (in whose freshman honors class I learned a great deal about reading and writing) went so far as to check out *Horseman* on permanent faculty loan from the Texas Christian University library, in what must have been a quixotic attempt to preserve the students' innocence. Even today, a preference for the staid rectitude of Elmer Kelton over the four-letter-word frankness of McMurtry is palpable among older West Texas academics.

The ongoing popularity of *Horseman, Pass By* is probably a huge surprise to its author, or perhaps he sees it as confirmation that English professors are sentimental and have limited imaginations. He has let it be known more than once that he regards the book that launched his career as something of a youthful embarrassment, calling it on one occasion "a piece of juvenilia." An inscription he wrote in a copy of the first edition reads, "This is about the sixth draft—I revised the book to death. L. McMurtry."

How the novel came about is a story in itself. The first glimmerings of *Horseman* appeared in McMurtry's undergraduate days at North Texas State College, today the University of North Texas. He had penned a bunch of short stories in his junior and senior years (1957 and 1958), but he destroyed sixty-three of them on the grounds that they weren't any good. (I know way too many writers in this state who, had they written those sixty-three stories, would have spent the rest of their lives trying to get them published.)

He did, however, think enough of a few of his stories to publish them in the student magazine *Avesta*. Among these was one that dealt with the destruction of a herd of infected cattle and

another that was about the death of an old rancher—the bones
of the novel that he would begin immediately upon graduating, in May 1958. Five drafts of the novel, the first dated May 26
through October 11, 1958, and the fifth dated August 11, 1960,
can be found at UT's Harry Ransom Center. McMurtry biled
them cabbage down, going from 447 pages in the first draft to
245 in the fifth. Some of the changes are interesting. A very long
scene set in a storm cellar brings all the characters together, and
while they wait out a possible tornado, many grievances are
aired. The whole scene in the storm cellar was cut—probably a
good decision. An interesting change was made in the naming
of Hud, the book's unprincipled anti-hero. Hud was originally
named Donny, which rhymed with the name of the narrator,
Lonnie, and so it would have been Donny and Lonnie, which
sounds like nothing so much as a pair of twin running backs at
some little Texas high school. Early on, Donny was changed to
the harder, meaner-sounding Hud (rhymes with "stud"). Lonnie,
who is something of a Western wimp, retained the soft name.
Somebody has floated the idea that Hud was named after Huddie
Ledbetter, but I've never been convinced of that one.

The first dedication did not stand either. The book is dedicated to McMurtry's parents "with gratitude and love." But
the original inscription was "To the working people of the
Texas earth; and to Grover Lewis; and to James Brown." The
late Grover Lewis, a talented writer and friend of McMurtry's,
taught philosophy at North Texas for a couple of years, where I
was one of his students. James Brown, a professor in the English
department who taught modern drama brilliantly, was another
teacher of mine.

The title as it is today was there from the first, and from
publication onward it has given readers trouble. According to
McMurtry, his friends called it variously "Horseman, Goodbye";
"Horseman, Ride By"; "Passing the Horseman"; and "So Long,
Horseman." One "dotty old lady" even dubbed it "The Four
Horsemen of the Alamo." Obviously these readers had not read
Yeats, because the title came from "Under Ben Bulben," a poem
that McMurtry doubtless read in one of his English classes at

North Texas, probably Dr. Joseph Logue's. Logue taught a course in modern British literature, and it was in his class where I first read Yeats. The phrase is from the poem's closing lines: "Cast a cold eye / On life, on death. / Horseman, pass by!" It was a highbrow, English major–type title and the last such in McMurtry's arsenal until the memoir *Walter Benjamin at the Dairy Queen,* which was really highbrow because only graduate students have heard of Mr. Benjamin (the last syllable of whose name rhymes with "queen").

Whatever McMurtry later thought about his debut novel, he seems to have been proud of it in 1962, when he received the Jesse Jones Award for the best book of fiction from the Texas Institute of Letters. In his acceptance remarks he revealed a maturity of literary understanding far beyond his years (he was then a ripe old 26), and, I dare say, far beyond the reach of the perennially geriatric TIL membership. He cited four national authors whose work he admired (James Jones, William Styron, Norman Mailer, and Jack Kerouac) and offered a vigorous defense of regional writing, but with the new—and to many TIL members, shocking—caveat that it was time for "frequently uncouth exactitude" to replace "genteel approximation." His target, he said, was the Mrs. Grundys of the Southwest, the prudes and censors who, incidentally, were as likely to be male as female. In his concluding remarks he returned to the theme of timid neo-puritanical censorship: "Mrs. Grundy is going to have to abandon her sidesaddle and show some petticoats yet, and it may be that that lady and a lot of other uneasy riders will one of these days get throwed." This speech has never been printed, but it is an amazing document and testimony to the youthful McMurtry's precocious brilliance.

The ground for *Horseman, Pass By* had been plowed earlier by a youth-oriented novel that had garnered a huge national following. I read the book entirely by accident, the way I read most literature when I was a teenager. McMurtry once wrote that he had grown up "in a bookless town in a bookless part of the state," but in fact that is where many of us grew up. My own town, Carrollton, was so bookless that about the only books in the school library were sports novels about sterling lads who attended prep schools and won the big game for Andover. That was okay; I read them all—and forgot them all. I can't remember a single title or author of boys' sports fiction from those lost days of the second Eisenhower administration, but I do remember a terrific book from that era. One day a friend of mine who was also a reader—that made two of us boys, at that time, in that place—was standing next to me at the checkout counter of the little library. "Read this," he said with a slight smirk, sliding a book over to me. "It's not about baseball; it's dirty. You'll like it." And I did; in fact, I thought *The Catcher in the Rye* was just about the best non-baseball novel I'd ever read.

Horseman, Pass By was our *Catcher in the Rye,* a Texas version, a little cruder, a little rawer. Holden Caulfield had to worry about sex in the city, but the boys in McMurtry's novel were decidedly rural. McMurtry introduced taboo material in a manner that one can only describe as poetic: "It hadn't been long since half the boys in the town had had a wild soiree with a blind heifer, out on a creek one cold night." "Soiree" is a real touch. Gertrude Beasley, back in 1925, had been the first Texas writer to tackle bestiality, but very few people had ever read *My First Thirty Years,* and it remains one of the rarest books in Texas literature. Beasley was also the first Texas writer to introduce that funny little word *penis,* but if I had to rate them, I'd say that nobody wrote about dating livestock better than Larry.

Later, I realized that among the many strengths of McMurtry's novel was its reflection of fifties culture. Lonnie, too, is a reader, a proto–English major in the making, and one of the books he admires is *From Here to Eternity,* which he purchased at the local drugstore. He likes James Jones's novel because its characters and ambience remind him of the lives of people in his county. Jones's novel was sensational in its day, the kind of book that was passed around in schools with the "dirty" passages flagged for those students who were never going to read a novel of such length or of any length, come to think of it. The drugstore is where I bought my paperback of *From Here to Eternity,* a book that school librarians dared not order in those days. Indeed there were so many things in McMurtry's book that rang true that we all awaited his next novel and his next, and they kept coming, down through the decades. Since that debut effort, McMurtry has published forty-one books and counting. And it all began, the long, distinguished career, with *Horseman, Pass By*.

2001

PART II *Culture*

MASTER CLASS

Year after year, I feel a deep indebtedness to J. Frank Dobie. The reason is quite simple: Dobie invented the course, Life and Literature of the Southwest, that brought me back to Texas from Pennsylvania. In 1976 I was hired by the Department of English at the University of Texas, from where I had earlier taken a Ph.D., to teach English 342, Dobie's old course. I have done so just about every semester since then, with the exception of exchange sojourns in France and Australia in the early 1990s. My training had been in mainstream American literature, and my interest in southwestern regional literature was a minor, personal, almost dilettantish interest.

The academy in those days was excited about adding film content to courses, in the hopes of building enrollments, and so I was hired specifically to offer a course in Western movies, just as, a few years earlier, the Penn English department had encouraged me to develop a course in Western movies for the same reason: to build up enrollments. I would never have thought of devising such a course on my own, but I quickly found the material interesting (it was like revisiting my childhood) and from such a course came conferences, essays, and two books dealing with the Western. I have always wondered what Dobie would have thought of the hijacking of his course to teach a form of representation of the Southwest, of Texas, that he was deeply suspicious of. Dobie was fifteen years old in 1903 when *The Great Train Robbery* was released, the same year, incidentally, that Andy Adams's *The Log of a Cowboy* was published as an antidote to the romantic melodrama of Owen Wister's *The Virginian,* published the year before. Dobie always celebrated Adams's realism and nearly always denigrated the shoot-em-ups that he saw from the silents to the talkies. The one exception was the longhorn cattle in *North of 36,* a 1924 silent film shot on location on a ranch near Houston. Dobie was thrilled that he could read the actual brands of the cattle and that they walked rather than ran at breakneck speed to Kansas the way they did in most oaters.

Teaching the Western was interesting until new technologies (video, etc.) and the decline of the genre to the point of near disappearance made the course no longer viable. The younger audience for Westerns vanished. I blame it all on Stephen Spielberg, but that's another story. In any event, I shifted the content to encompass the Far West as well as the Southwest and taught it for a number of years as essentially a course in the literature of the American West. In fact, at one point the English department wanted to discard Dobie's original title of the course in favor of "Literature of the American West." Through some kind of bureaucratic snafu, the title was never changed, and I was glad about that, as I believe Dobie would have been. At some point in the late '80s or early '90s, I don't recall exactly when, I refocused the course with a vengeance: though the title remained the same, the course was now redesigned in my syllabus and approach, as a course devoted to Texas literature. To my mind Texas was the quintessential southwestern state and its literature was rich enough to justify the narrowing (or expansion, if you look at it another way) to concentrate entirely on Texas writing.

The course begins with a question: Who was J. Frank Dobie? The answers increasingly are "I don't have a clue." The best answer, that is, the worst, that I ever received was from a few years back, when a student wrote: "J. Frank Dobie—the man after which Dobie Mall is named. He was, I think, a Texas Ranger with some authority. He was an outspoken Racist. I learned that in a class, The History of Mexican Americans in the U.S."

So begins the process of bringing the largely forgotten historical figure to life. It was at the tail end of the 1920s that Dobie proposed a new course to be taught in the Department of English at the University of Texas. A lowly M.A. instructor with no aspirations to acquire a doctorate, Dobie wanted to offer a course on southwestern literature. Immediately he ran into strong opposition. As the story goes, the Ph.D.s solemnly declared that there was no such thing. Dobie's riposte became part of his legend: "Well, there's plenty of life in the Southwest, so I'll just teach the life." Dobie, incidentally, did not have much use for Ph.D.s, arguing that in their theses they "merely transfer bones from one graveyard to another."

To be fair, however, the old dons in the English department had a point. In 1929 American literature itself was only beginning to cut into the dominance of British and classical literature in the colleges and universities around the country. Certainly the Southwest as a literary region would seem a hard sell to professors skeptical of adding national literature to the curriculum. Dobie well understood what he was up against: "Some of the departments here have no more sympathy for the life of the Southwest than they have for life in Patagonia."

Happily, Dobie's proposal coincided with a burst of creative literary energy in the Southwest. In 1930, for example, two southwestern books racked up Pulitzer Prizes: Santa Fe–based author Oliver La Farge's novel *Laughing Boy* and Marquis James's biography of Texas hero Sam Houston, *The Raven*. In Texas, things were astir as well. Katherine Anne Porter's *Flowering Judas* was published to widespread acclaim, and Dobie's own *Coronado's Children* achieved national standing by being picked as both a Literary Guild and a Book-of-the-Month selection.

In any event, Dobie prevailed and got his course up and running in the spring semester of 1930. He would offer it regularly for the next decade and it would continue in other hands through the century and into the next. The manner in which Dobie taught the class can be gleaned from a surviving document from the spring semester of 1940—a compilation of the best work done by members of the class. In May the students put together a bound mimeographed anthology with a title in the form of a cattle brand: E342 [*note: the E is on its back with the three lines sticking up—a Lazy E*]. The title page described the work as "A Collection of Stray Mavericks Caught, Roped, and Branded by Members of the 'Big Corral' (English 342: Life and Literature of the Southwest)." A student named William H. Cleveland, Jr., was listed as the "Foreman," and the "Boss O' the Outfit" was, naturally, J. Frank Dobie. Sixty-nine pages long, the anthology brought together the work of thirty-nine student contributors from a total of 107 class members.

In a brief preface, Dobie, the "chief ramrod," enthusiastically endorsed his experience of teaching the course that spring: "Riding with you three mornings a week in the room numbered 201 under 'the Doric wheat elevator' has generally been bully business for me." (The Doric wheat elevator was Dobie's characteristic disparagement of the recently erected UT Tower, which he never missed an opportunity to mock.)

The preface went on to defend, as Dobie did many times in his writings, the rationale for studying the art of a particular region. Wrote Dobie: "I have not ceased to din into your ears the idea that any literature, art, architecture, or even music that the Southwest can hope to achieve, will, if it is 'authentic,' reflect the backgrounds of its setting." Then he took a familiar swipe at the Littlefield fountain, arguing that the sculptor should have depicted burros or mustangs instead of winged horses. One thing about Dobie: he didn't mind repeating himself and when he disliked something he kept reminding everybody of why they should too.

Dobie, who never met a Western metaphor he didn't like, certainly impressed his rhetoric upon his erstwhile scholars. Student work was arranged in categories that might have come from a Dobie book: "Critters in the Southwest"; "The Pioneers"; "Those Hero Folks"; "Dust, Quartz, and Bullion"; "Ridin' Herd"; and "Hunter's Stew."

As for his students' scribblings, they all sounded like little Dobies. The titles of the individual pieces included "Cougar Tales My Grandma Told," "The Story of Juan Torres," "Dulco, the Cutting Horse," "Down the Road Lived Bigfoot Wallace," "Buried Treasure in Central Texas," and "The Cowboy's Philosophy."

Dobie the literary and curriculum pioneer was leading his charges into the still fertile field of frontier folklore. His students could interview grandparents and other old-timers who went right back to the thrilling days of yesteryear. Nineteenth-century history was as close as granddad's rocking chair.

Because of the newness of the subject and the scarcity of texts—remember, this was long before the paperback revolution—Dobie did not have a core set of works, a canon, that everybody read. In effect he was trying to figure out if there *was* a canon, a generally agreed-upon consensus as to what the best works were. To this end Dobie assembled and added to, as the years went by, an annotated list of books that he considered useful.

One such mimeographed compilation, for example, was put together in 1936, under the title "Life and Literature of the Southwest: An Incomplete Guide to Books on Texas and the Southwest." Here Dobie made the case for his subject in his usually combative manner. Castigating Harvard and the "sheep-like makers of textbooks" for emphasizing the Puritan writers whom he considered "dreary creatures," he wrote, "I rebel at having the tradition, the spirit, the meaning of the soil to which I belong utterly neglected by academicians and at the same time having the Cotton Mather kind of thing taught." One imagines that this point of view went over very well with students who had struggled through Jonathan Edwards and the rest of the merry Puritans.

The "Incomplete Guide" eventuated, in 1942, in book publication of *Guide to Life and Literature of the Southwest,* followed ten years later by a second edition "Revised and Enlarged in Both Knowledge and Wisdom." By then Dobie had won the battle for regionalism but now tempered his claims considerably. In "A Preface with Some Revised Ideas" he expressed dismay at "provincial inbreeding," which led to chauvinistic championing of the second-rate. "I am sorry," he wrote, "to see writings of the Southwest substituted for noble and beautiful and wise literature to which all people everywhere are inheritors." In another passage he assayed a life's work in these terms: "No informed person would hold that the Southwest can claim any considerable body of *pure literature* as its own." The one concession he was willing to make was the one with which he had begun, back in 1930: at least the Southwest had a "distinct cultural inheritance, full of life and drama."

By the time of Dobie's death in 1964, new voices were abroad in the land, and Dobie read them right up to the end, although they did not always sing to him: Larry McMurtry, Edward Abbey, John Graves, Billy Lee Brammer, Edwin Shrake, and others. Here is what he thought of Brammer's *The Gay Place:* "We are in the middle of politics for 175,000 words, and nobody actually ever does anything but drink and drink & drink to boredom & screw, & screw & screw to death—the great governor's climax." He found similar problems with Edwin Shrake's *But Not for Love:* "Over drinking of everything but water. Prolonged drunk talk gets boresome . . . Pages & pages of talk that reveal nothing but more drinking, more smoking." It was Graves he liked the best. *Goodbye to a River* was squarely in the Dobie-Bedichek-Webb tradition.

The course he invented rolled on and was imitated at other colleges and universities in the Southwest and the West. Dobie's attempts at canon-formation influenced writers like A. C. Greene, whose "The Fifty Best Texas Books," excerpted in *Texas Monthly* (August 1981), stimulated useful discussion for a decade or more.

Now Dobie is a statue, enshrined in bronze, but his course flourishes, and it is in the classroom where the canon gets defined every time a professor draws up a list of required readings. At the University of Texas, Rolando Hinojosa-Smith and I regularly offer sections of 342. Without any concerted effort, the texts we use represent a pretty firm consensus. We usually teach various combinations of Larry McMurtry, Katherine Anne Porter, George Sessions Perry, Américo Paredes, Cormac McCarthy, and Rolando Hinojosa-Smith. Authors taught singly include John Graves, Sandra Cisneros, Tomás Rivera, J. Frank Dobie, Billy Lee Brammer, Edwin Shrake, Peter Gent, C. C. White, and many others. Beneficiaries of the paperback revolution, we are yet dependent on publishers' whims as to what is kept in print and what is not.

Were Dobie to come back today, he would find the course much changed perhaps, but he would also find the same ongoing critical effort, in Matthew Arnold's words, "to learn and propagate the best that is known and thought in the world." In this case, of course, the world is the Southwest.

2003

FALLEN HEROES

Like the Alamo, the Texas Rangers embody the idea of Texas exceptionalism, the notion that the Lone Star State (there it is again) is different from the rest of the United States. The most famous book about those doughty defenders of truth, justice, and the American Way is Walter P. Webb's *The Texas Rangers: A Century of Frontier Defense* (1935). Among many fans of Ranger lore, it is still the gold standard. But with the passage of time, Webb's book is beginning to seem what it is, a somewhat dated and culturally nostalgic celebration of Old Texas.

The problems with this particular Texas classic are multiple: its narrative is scattered and lacks unity; it tends to lapse into anecdotage (as do many of the works of the Big Three, Dobie/Webb/Bedichek); it presents the Rangers as demigods; and as novelist Rolando Hinojosa-Smith has said, it is virtually a "life of saints." In the process of lionizing the Rangers, it whitewashes their excesses, offering excuses and justifications for illegal actions such as torture and murder.

The book's most significant shortcoming by far is its racist rhetoric. Webb's hierarchy of race reflects an all-too-common late nineteenth-century misreading of Darwin that carried over into the twentieth century. At the top are the Anglos, and at the very top of the Anglo heap are the Texas Rangers. (Anglo outlaws, however bad, are exempted from racist characterization.) In Webb's color-coded world, the Plains Indians rate higher than the Mexicans. The Comanches and Apaches are almost noble at times, living close to Mother Earth as they do, but they are also called "savages" repeatedly. One thing for sure, they were not some pantywaist squash raisers in East Texas like the Caddos and Cherokees. Webb relates a story about an 1880 Ranger patrol in West Texas that sticks in the mind. Chasing an Apache raiding party, the Rangers came upon a herd of stolen cattle that had been left behind. The cattle were alive, but hunks of meat had been ripped from their bodies by the warriors eager for a little steak alfresco.

The outlaws and the Native Americans have never offered a response or critique of Webb, but Mexican Americans have returned heavy fire and continue to do so. The first serious challenge to Webb's version of Ranger history came from the late writer and University of Texas professor, Américo Paredes, who hailed from the lower Rio Grande Valley, where Ranger depredations had been most numerous and flagrant. Paredes's pioneering study of Mexican American culture, *"With His Pistol in His Hand": A Border Ballad and Its Hero* (1958), drew attention to overtly racist language in both *The Texas Rangers* and another Webb classic, *The Great Plains.* In the latter, Webb characterizes the Mexican Indian as one "whose blood, when compared with that of the Plains Indian, was as ditch water." Every Hispanic who has read the book can quote this line from memory. In the Rangers book Webb trafficked in the grossest of stereotypes, announcing that there is "a cruel streak in the Mexican nature."

Today it's mainly history buffs who are interested in the nineteenth-century Rangers. But a later chapter of their history—the Border War of 1915–1916—still resonates. The basic outline is that in January 1915 a revolutionary manifesto called the *Plan de San Diego* was issued in South Texas. It called for a coalition of Mexican Americans, blacks, Indians, and rather strangely, Japanese, to rise up against the American oppressors. One of its most shocking provisions called for the killing of all Anglo males aged sixteen and over. But nothing happened immediately. Then, in the early summer of that year, armed raiders attacked Anglo ranch houses, burned bridges, and created a wave of fear and terror along the border. Anglo reprisals followed, and the Rangers were particularly ferocious in their methods of punishing the *Sediciosos* (the revolutionaries) and the innocent.

Much of the recent coverage seems to have been spurred by the publication of *Revolution in Texas: How a Forgotten Rebellion and Its Bloody Suppression Turned Mexicans into Americans* (2004) by Benjamin Huber Johnson, and by Kirby Warnock's *Border Bandits* (2004), a documentary film based on the murder of two innocent Mexican Americans during that period. Articles in the *New York Times,* the *Dallas Morning News,* and other newspapers throughout the United States ran stories based on the revelations in Johnson's book.

Johnson expresses a sense of amazement at never having heard of the Troubles of 1915–1916: "The uprising was thus violent, large, and had important consequences. Then why had neither I nor my parents, all of us natives of Texas and products of its school system, even heard of it?" The answer is simple: (1) they had not read Webb, and (2) their history teachers were probably coaches. For all of his defenses of Ranger behavior in *The Texas Rangers,* Webb actually devotes several pages regarding the *Plan de San Diego* and its bloody aftermath. In sections titled "Dead Men on the Rio Grande" and "The Rangers and Their Bandit Troubles," he writes of the "death of hundreds of Mexicans, many of them innocent, at the hands of the local posses, peace officers, and Texas Rangers." Surprisingly for those who always criticize Webb for his Rangers bias, he condemns their activities in quite strong terms: "In the orgy of bloodshed that followed [the raids by Mexicans and Mexican Americans], the Texas Rangers played a prominent part, and one of which many members of the force have been heartily ashamed."

Webb's estimate of the number of Mexicans and Mexican Americans slain in South Texas placed the death toll between "five hundred and five thousand, but the actual number can never be known." That higher number has proved irresistible to the daily press in the wake of 9/11. In a syndicated newspaper column written in 2004, Ruben Navarrette Jr. stated: "Estimates of casualties clock in at more than 3,000 or about the same number of people who died in the terrorist attacks of Sept. 11, 2001." Despite the drama of the higher number, no convincing evidence or documentation has ever been brought forward to demonstrate such levels of carnage. Other historians, such as Charles H. Harris III and Luis R. Sadler, in their meticulously researched *The Texas Rangers and the Mexican Revolution: The Bloodiest Decade, 1910–1920* (2004) conclude that about three hundred Mexican and Mexican American people were killed, as compared to twenty Anglos. The emotional toll exacted upon Mexican American culture in South Texas during those years is perhaps best caught in Américo Paredes's novel, *George Washington Gomez,* published in 1992.

This sorry chapter in Ranger history led directly to hearings in the state legislature in 1919 and to the issuance of a largely unread and unpublished report. In fact, publicity surrounding the legislative investigation in 1919 is what gave Webb the idea of writing about the Rangers. The report also led to the enactment of some needed reforms in the structure and mission of the Ranger organization.

The closing chapters of Webb's book introduce a personal dimension that somewhat weakens the book. First of all, he devotes a whole chapter to his friend Frank Hamer, made famous by carrying out the bloody ambush of Bonnie and Clyde. And in another chapter, "Some Adventures of a Texas Historian," Webb recalls the glorious time in 1924 when he joined a group of Rangers for an extended trip along the border from the Big Bend area to the Rio Grande Valley, on horseback, camping out, armed and dangerous, just like the old-time Rangers. He even participated in the capture of a bootlegging operation (this was during Prohibition, remember). There is a funny story about Webb amongst the Rangers that appears in Necah Furman's *Walter Prescott Webb: His Life and Impact* (1976). Not wanting to appear the tenderfoot who would be the butt of practical jokes, Webb survived the outdoors life unscathed, but later in a little café in West Texas, when the Rangers stuck him with the bill for breakfast, he forked over two dollar bills and asked the waitress, "How much will you take off for cash?" she fired back, "Everything but my shoes, Baldy." The Rangers laughed all the way back to Austin.

Webb's book ends in 1935, the year that the Rangers were absorbed into the Department of Public Safety. Webb thought that the Rangers were going to disappear, but they did not. They retained their individual identity as well as all the mythic baggage, positive and negative. Near the end of the twentieth century, the Rangers had morphed into more of a multiculturally composite group rather than a band of hard-core white males. By 1998, in a force of 105 Rangers, there were two women, six African Americans, fourteen Hispanics, and one Asian American. The Rangers were beginning to look like the face of Texas, of America. The methods were changing, too. No more six-gun justice, no more ambushes like that of Bonnie and Clyde. The last publicized capture of a desperado by a Texas Ranger occurred in 1999, when Ángel Maturino Reséndiz (aka Rafael Reséndez-Ramírez), the railroad killer, surrendered to a Texas Ranger, Sgt. Drew Carter. Instead of a gun, the Ranger's weapon was a telephone. He had called Reséndiz's family members, urging them to persuade the fugitive to give himself up.

Just as the Ranger organization changed, so did Webb's opinion of his book. In comparison with his most important works (*The Great Plains, The Great Frontier*), he regarded it as merely a "competent journeyman's job." He had come to believe that his picture of the Rangers, particularly their notorious activities in South Texas, had failed sufficiently to consider the Mexican and Mexican American point of view. He intended to make some changes in a new edition, telling his friend Frank Wardlaw, director of the University of Texas Press, that "if a man can't grow in thirty years, he may as well be dead." But a fatal auto wreck in 1963 canceled any chance of emending the record in the edition that the University of Texas would reissue two years later with an adulatory introduction by that other Lone Star Icon, President Lyndon B. Johnson.

Although Webb is still regarded as the greatest historian the state has produced, *The Texas Rangers* is not the book on which to make such a case. There are flashes of excellent writing, some solid research, and some well-told stories. But ultimately the book seems dated, like a lot of narratives confined to Texas materials and not connected to a national narrative. It's why the word *Texana* was invented.

2005

This reevaluation of a famous Texas book drew some vigorous responses from readers of *Texas Monthly*. One high school coach-teacher, who otherwise liked the piece, took umbrage at the crack I'd made about Texas history being largely taught by coaches. The umbraged one called for me to apologize to all coach-teachers in Texas high schools. I have yet to issue that apology, and I find that many of my current students raise their hands when I ask how many of them "studied" history from football coaches in high school.

But the strongest reaction was from a rancher who described what I had written as a "hate-attack against the eminent Texas historian Walter Prescott Webb." He went on to condemn my commentary as "Really vicious. Eye-gouging, groin-kicking. Way overboard." The letter concluded: "The problem with *Texas Monthly* is that its head, Mike Levy, is a New York Jew and your values are those of a New York Jew, not Texan values."

THE PITS

I once wrote a biography, beginning at the beginning, and upon completing the first chapter, fired it off to my agent, who promptly replied that he couldn't sell a book on the strength of someone's childhood. So I flashed forward to a dramatic moment in the life I was chronicling, and the book was on its way. That was long ago and in another century, and only a few years later everything changed and it became possible, even desirable, to write only about childhood, preferably one's own and especially if one had been abused. Sexual abuse was best, but in its stead there was always derivative Dickensian-level suffering—the formula of *Angela's Ashes.*

In Texas in the nineties the memoir, aping national tendencies, thrived. Marion Winik wrote about her marriage to a gay man felled by AIDS—he was seen around town dying by degrees. Lars Eighner lived in a ditch, and when he wrote about it, people responded. It was something new; Austin literati took him out to dinner. Not since the lives of saints had suffering been so admired. Being interviewed on National Public Radio confirmed the stigmata of significant anguish. Winik even made it onto *Oprah,* the sweepstakes of superior feeling (this was before the eponymous diva's forays into spiritualism and theosophy). Prior to such outpourings of emotional turmoil, Texas memoirs had tended toward the elegiac: in the most famous, an academic paddled a canoe down a river that he thought was going to be dammed and entertained deep thoughts about philosophy, history, and local weather conditions.

By far the greatest success in the new confessional mode, however, belonged to Mary Karr, the Peck Professor of English at Syracuse University. In the wildly acclaimed and best-selling *The Liars' Club* (1995), Karr told everything there apparently was to tell about her redneck, refinery-trash family adrift in imaginary Leechfield, Texas, a small, smelly, petrochemically challenged burg somewhere between Beaumont and Port Arthur: Janis Joplin and Jimmy Johnson country. Karr's book hit a nerve; feminists got down with the author's bad self—a sassy, brassy, dirty-talking, hip-leftist, kick-ass NOW sister-in-the-making. Molly Ivins and Ann Richards had paved the way. Everybody was ready to read about How It Was growing up female in good-ol'-boy country. "You go, girl!" rang like a chorus in discussion groups at the big book chains.

The author of a couple of mainly invisible books of poetry, Karr was now highly visible; she was everywhere. In 1996 she came to the annual meeting of the Texas Institute of Letters, held in Houston that year, to accept the Carr P. Collins Prize for the best nonfiction book of the year. Her mama and sister were in attendance too. They made a good-looking threesome; they might have lunched at the River Oaks Grill that day and spent the afternoon shopping at the Galleria.

In her remarks Karr allowed as how she was already at work on son—or, rather, daughter—of *The Liars' Club*. It would be called *Cherry,* she said, which drew an approving twitter, and it was going to be harder to write than the first one because everybody had done so many drugs nobody could remember what had happened. Big salvo of laughter. I recall thinking, "Why don't you just make it up, the way you probably did *The Liars' Club,* because who can remember all those details from one's childhood?" But I remind myself: What do you know? You haven't been through therapy, a process that is famous for constructing memories of events—always traumatic—that may or may not have happened.

From what Karr said in Houston, I concluded, quite wrongly as it turned out, that *Cherry* was going to be about the years of her youth after leaving home: the drug scene, Vietnam, the

seventies. But that is not the case at all. After a feverish pro-
logue about the angst of Departure, the book returns to the
old familiar ground of *The Liars' Club,* the war-torn landscape
of the battlin' Karrs. So what we have is Liars' Club II, sans one
of the best characters, the author's dad. He's still around but is
no longer indispensable to the little girl he calls Pokey. Puberty
intervenes. "I want titties, goddamn it, Daddy. Not some bra,"
Pokey blurts out in one family council. No wonder Dad drops
out, goes fishing.

It was Tolstoy, I believe, who wrote that all functional families are alike, but a dysfunctional family is dysfunctional after
its own fashion. Yes, but dysfunctionality is not always interesting, vide any episode of *Jenny Jones.* The chaotic daily life of the
Karrs—a "distressed" family, in Karr's usage—does not need to
be revisited but it is, filtered now through the narcissism (understandable but tedious nonetheless) of young Pokey as she colt-
ishly staggers into adolescence, confronting the big issues. Will
she grow breasts? Yes. Will she have sex with John Cleary, her
first big crush? No. But she does kiss him, and for Karr a kiss
is not just a kiss: "Suddenly, I know so much. I understand
about waves and cross tides and how jellyfish float and why
rivers empty themselves in the Gulf. I understand the undulat-
ing movement of the stingray on *Sea Hunt* and the hard forward
muscle of the shark." I hope she's trying to be funny, but if so I
don't see it. I think this is what she thinks, or rather, *feels.*

When Karr's language about sex isn't faux poetic, it's potty-
mouth. At eleven precocious Pokey dreams of a "bona fide
boning." Things that break or don't work are invariably called
"broke-dick." Mom talks to her daughter about female genitalia
and sex acts using vulgarities that are still, even in these enlight-
ened times, shocking. Mother and daughter give each other the
finger. At one point Pokey thinks portentously, "Of actual john-
sons I had little awareness"—a sentence that, strictly from a sty-
listic viewpoint, seems ridiculous. Later, imagining the boy she
will eventually choose to sleep with, she thinks, "You get the
feeling that, unleashed, this tender boy would throw you to the

earth and boff you into guacamole." No thanks, I don't feel like Mexican food today.

The book's structure limps along (I started to say in broke-dick fashion) from grade to grade. Chapter six begins, "Seventh grade actually starts for me . . ." and chapter seven, "Sometime during the eighth grade . . . ," and then, almost halfway through the book, we read, "Suddenly it's ninth grade," and we want to shout, "Whaddaya mean 'suddenly'?" We're on a Bataan death march here, forced to relive every grade year by year, summer by summer, the molasses-slow progress of Pokey from child to sub-teen to teen. God, will it ever end? Late in the book a cop tells her to "Shut the f— up," and you think, "Hey, not a bad idea."

Karr's mouthy, counterculture, wiseass persona thinks far too highly of her "outlaw" self. At one point she writes, "you've been floating along pretty much on your own, especially since Daddy vanished into wherever Daddy goes to, and Lecia took her right-wing turn just as you hooked to the left." Very proud she is of that left turn, presented here as a noble action, a natural outgrowth of her parents' Depression-dyed, yellow-dog Demo-cratic party hatred of Republicans. But her sister, Lecia, targeted here as a right-winger and mocked in *The Liars' Club* for having voted for Ronald Reagan twice—and triply branded for being married to the "Rice Baron"—is arguably the sanest of the Karrs, the only one to have a lick of sense. It's a relief to read about Lecia, a pleasure to get away from Pokey for a while, just as it is when the interesting, intellectual Meredith, a newcomer to Leechfield High, is introduced late in the book.

The Liars' Club is superior to *Cherry* because it contains well-drawn portraits of Other People: father, mother, grandmother. Contrary to what Sartre wrote, Hell is not other people; it's adolescent narcissism à la *Cherry*. A girlfriend who deliber-ately drops Pokey does so, she says, because Pokey thinks she is smarter than everybody else. Karr recognizes—nay, embraces—the truth of this claim. But she isn't smarter. She's just more "sensitive"—or thinks she is. It's no accident that her favorite poet, early on, is the doyen of teenage rebellion, e. e. cummings, whose radical typography endears him to the young and masks his often sentimental themes: spring is good, love is good, salesmen are shits, and so on. To give Karr credit, she reads a lot of literature as a youngster and sprinkles her text with allusions to famous works and authors, unnamed so that her audience — composed mainly, one imagines, of college-educated readers — can enjoy little spasms of self-congratulatory pleasure in recognizing cummings, Eliot, Hawthorne, and "The Lottery."

Eighteen months before graduation — there's that school time line again — she begins to smoke a lot of dope and quickly moves on to trendier modes of achieving chemical nirvana — psilocybin, hallucinogens, but not heroin; like a good girl, she tried that only once. As things begin to grow drug-hazy, Karr introduces the refrain, "Who could have seen it coming?" Well, nearly anybody in 1971. Her sister certainly did. Lecia, rightwinger that she is, sees through "Hate"-Ashbury first thing. Only Dopey-Pokey never does. Not even after she spends a night in the Kountze County jail, arrested along with her fellow skinny-dipping, hippie-dippy midnight tokers.

The book has a big epiphany in store for us. Near the end, Karr finds herself in another tight spot, in a backwoods black blues joint where she confronts some down-and-outers she's not prepared to deal with: a huge black woman who exudes menace and a striptease dancer who may in fact be a man and who, observed by Karr in the unspeakably sordid toilet, stabs a hypodermic needle of junk into her/his neck. This walk on the wild side scares the bejeebers out of Karr and sends her back pell-mell to rejoin her cowboy dad, histrionic mom, and Republican sister. Then she goes to see the sage Meredith and delivers the great truth she has learned: "There's no place like home."

Robert Graves, the author of the classic World War I memoir *Goodbye to All That,* lived to be ninety and wrote 120 books, only one of which, the first, was about himself. He reckoned that his life from the Great War onward had been devoid of anything of autobiographical interest. Of course it was Graves's conviction that memoirs should deal with one's encounters with history, significant public events. That assumption has long since given way to the current state of things, an infantilization of culture in which anybody who survives childhood can make—or make up—a book out of it.

In the end, I am reminded of the words that the woman speaks to her husband at the end of Hemingway's great story, "Hills Like White Elephants." She has agreed to have the abortion that her husband wants her to have, but she is tired of hearing him talk about it, and she tells him, "Would you please please please please please stop talking."

2000

A lot of memories attach to this piece. I was teaching in the University of Texas Oxford Program in England when I got the assignment from *Texas Monthly*. Since I didn't have easy access to a computer, I wrote it the old-fashioned way, in longhand, then went to an Internet café where, amidst deafening Euro-trash music, I typed in the copy. Perhaps being in England gave me a certain distance and clarity; I'm pretty sure it did. In any event, I said what I wanted to say and what I felt about this book. I called it "Pokey's Progress," but I had several other titles in mind: Karr Trouble, Karr Wreck, Bad Karrma, etc. *Texas Monthly,* however, went with "The Pits," playing off of the book's title, *Cherry.* "Cherry Bomb" would have been an option, too.

I was back in the states by the time the piece came out, and the reactions were lively, to say the least. Some people loved it, and some hated it. Among those who hated it was Mary Karr her own self. Karen Olsson, an Austin-based journalist, gave Karr an opening in an interview in the *The Texas Observer* (December 8, 2000) by asking her what she thought of "the weirdly resentful and personal article about the book that ran in *Texas Monthly.*" Karr responded by saying, "I just think the guy who wrote it didn't like the book, he doesn't like me, he doesn't like the idea of me, he doesn't like how I look, he doesn't like how my mother looks, doesn't like how my sister looks, doesn't like women, doesn't like . . . I really was kind of shocked. I didn't read the whole thing. Seemed like a guy who was disappointed with the way the world had treated him." For the record, I thought the Karr family—mother and two daughters—looked great the time I saw them at the TIL meeting in Houston. But it is absolutely true that I didn't like the book. Incidentally, my wife, Betsy Berry, wrote a feisty letter to the *Observer* characterizing our life together as "healthy, happy, adventurous, funny, and altogether wonderful." Correct on all points.

Karr has now published her third memoir, *Lit: A Memoir* (2009). She has only four to go to catch Proust.

ACCENTUATE
THE NEGATIVE

Fifteen years after her death, Patricia Highsmith is finally coming into her own in America. W. W. Norton has reissued her entire body of work, and the dimensions
of her oeuvre continue to impress. Highsmith can no longer be
thought of as merely a gifted genre writer. Her range of interests and accomplishments far surpasses the limitations of a particular type of fiction. Highsmith resisted being branded, preferring to think of herself as a novelist rather than a crime writer.
But American publishers wanted labels. Thus her first book,
Strangers on a Train, was published as a "novel of suspense." And so
to avoid another label—"lesbian-book writer"—Highsmith used
a pseudonym for her second novel, *The Price of Salt,* a sensational
narrative of an affair between two women.

It is time to stop categorizing Highsmith in either of these
terms. Perhaps Graham Greene, a devoted admirer of her work,
put it best when he called her a "poet of apprehension." Indeed
she is. To read a Highsmith novel is to suspend one's moral judg-
ments. She irresistibly persuades the reader to side with killers
and other amoral characters. Her world is perverse and curiously
animated: As though they were cartoon objects, guns "look"
at their targets (in the forties Highsmith wrote copy for comic
books), and characters are propelled by unstable psychologies.
Much of her fiction reminds me of Flannery O'Connor without the theology. Highsmith was a master of the macabre as
well, especially in her short stories. A typical one, "The Hand,"
opens this way: "A young man asked a father for his daughter's

hand, and received it in a box—her left hand." For such a dark lady, Highsmith had a dark sense of humor as well. She howled with laughter, for example, at a printing error that listed Graham Greene's *Travels with My Aunt* as *Travels with My Cunt*. She thought that was about the funniest thing she'd ever seen. Late in her career she published a volume of short stories about pets killing their owners. She had odd proclivities: she loved snails and liked to carry them around in her purse and take them out in restaurants to muck around on the table. A wonderful writer, she didn't believe in anything, and in her free-floating misanthropy she approaches Swiftian levels of disgust toward feelings that most people cherish.

Thanks to Andrew Wilson's excellent biography, *Beautiful Shadow: A Life of Patricia Highsmith* (2003), we now know where all of this anger came from: it came from Texas. According to Highsmith, who was born in 1921, her essential character was formed by age six, and those first six years were spent in Fort Worth. Trouble began early, in the womb. Her mother, who eventually turned into a kind of monster and lived nearly forever, tried to abort her by drinking turpentine. Later both mother and daughter thought it was funny that Patricia grew up to like the smell of turpentine. Jay B. Plangman, her biological father, was not around; he bailed on the marriage several months before Patricia was born, and she did not meet him until she was twelve. Her mother soon married Stanley Highsmith, and although Patricia took her stepfather's name, she never liked the man himself. In fact, she dreamed about killing him.

Fortunately there were things about her early years in Fort Worth that were positive. She loved her maternal grandmother, Willie Mae, who gave her the kind of unconditional emotional support that was always absent from her mother's modus operandi, which consisted of undermining and carpet bombing her daughter's hopes and dreams. She liked the close-to-nature feel of the frontier city and enjoyed visits to a ranch that relatives owned in Weatherford, where she rode horses, a pastime she once said was "perhaps the only respect in which I resemble a Texan." Friends disagreed. They found her in many ways Texan to the core. She was "very conservative," remembered one, and her politics in later life were kind of wacky. She was ardently pro-Palestine and anti-Israel, and in 1992 she voted for Ross Perot for president. She disliked Jews and blacks, but then, as she once said, she didn't like anybody. Wilson writes that toward the end of her life she dressed like an "off-duty cowboy: 34-inch-waist Levis, sneakers and neckerchiefs." She liked Southern cooking—cornbread, collard greens, black-eyed peas, and such—until the day she died, in 1995, far away from Fort Worth, in Switzerland.

Highsmith's mother and stepfather moved from Fort Worth to New York City in 1927, but they returned to Texas off and on over the next few years. Wherever they were, the parents quarreled a lot, creating anxiety and stress in their young daughter. Looking back on her family life, she pronounced it a "little hell." In 1933 the couple separated for a time, and Highsmith, then twelve, was stashed in Fort Worth with her grandmother to attend school for a year. It was an act of abandonment that her mother never explained or justified, and Highsmith remembered that time as the "saddest" of her life.

The next year she returned to New York with her reunited but still squabbling parents. When she was fourteen, her mother asked her point-blank, "Are you a lesbian? You are beginning to make noises like one." By age sixteen, following heterosexual dates arranged by her mother, she was able to report that a goodnight kiss from a boy she'd had dinner with was "like falling into a bucket of oysters." She also slept with a boy that year, as a kind of experiment, and hated it.

After graduating from high school, in 1938, she spent a few months in Fort Worth with her beloved grandmother, and during this time she got to know her biological father a bit. This too was strange and unsettling, as Plangman seemed to want to seduce her, and there were, she later wrote to her stepfather, some "lingering kisses." He also showed her some pornographic pictures. Is it any wonder that Patricia Highsmith had a low opinion of family life and that she possessed one of the keenest senses of perversity of any modern writer?

After high school she attended Barnard College, where she wrote for the student literary magazine. She had some good luck early on. In 1948 her new pal Truman Capote got her into the famed Yaddo arts colony, in upstate New York, where one of her fellow aspiring writers was Flannery O'Connor. There Highsmith spent crucial, formative time working on *Strangers on a Train* (1950).

She got lucky again when Alfred Hitchcock decided to film it. All traces of Texas are stripped away in the movie, but reading the novel recently, I was surprised by how saturated it is with her memories of Texas and the West. The plot is simple: A wastrel psychopath, Charles Anthony Bruno, talks a promising young architect, Guy Haines, into killing Bruno's father in return for Bruno's killing Guy's wife.

The first half of the novel has several scenes set in the fictional Metcalf, Texas, which appears to be based on Fort Worth. While Guy is in Mexico visiting his girlfriend, Anne, Bruno goes to Metcalf and tracks down Guy's wife, Miriam. "He liked Texas, Guy's state! Everybody looked happy and full of energy." Trailing her to Lake Metcalf's Kingdom of Fun, a gaudy amusement park, he rides a merry-go-round horse and shouts, "Yeeeehooo! I'm a Texan!" Shortly afterward, he finds Miriam and chokes her to death. Then he needs a drink, and somebody at a bar gives him a shot of rye: "It was rough as Texas going down, but sweet when it got there."

Highsmith's next novel, *The Price of Salt,* also has a strong sense of the West in it, though nothing of Texas per se. Published in 1952, it garnered respectful reviews, and the next year, Bantam Books's 25-cent edition (advertised on the title page as "The Novel of a Love Society Forbids") sold like crazy. There are many things to say about this wonderful book, but I will concentrate on only one motif: the road trip through the West taken by the beautiful, upper-middle-class, thirty-something married woman, Carol, and the nineteen-year-old salesgirl-set designer, Therese, who is madly in love with her. Some critics are convinced that the women's flight of passion and their pursuit by a detective hired by Carol's husband was the inspiration for a similar tale of obsession, Vladimir Nabokov's *Lolita*. I would suggest some further echoes of Highsmith's see-America plot line in Jack Kerouac's *On the Road* and the film *Thelma and Louise*.

In Highsmith's subsequent fiction, the Texas traces largely disappear. She tended to set her books in locales where she was living, in New York or, increasingly, in Europe. But no matter where she went, Texas, in the form of her mother, was always there with her, a succubus she could not escape. Finally, in 1963, she moved to Europe for good.

In 1970 and 1974 she traveled to Fort Worth to visit her mother, who was slipping into Alzheimer's but would live until the age of 95, dying at last just four years before her daughter. In 1986 Highsmith wrote a short story, "No End in Sight," about her mother, and though it was set in Oklahoma, it was really Texas. It began: "She lies now, certainly a hundred and ninety, some say two hundred and ten, and with no end in sight." The story is surely the ghastliest fiction ever penned by a daughter about a mother living in a nursing home.

Highsmith made her last visit to Texas in 1992, staying at her cousin's ranch in Weatherford. She wrote what may be her final pronouncement on her native state in a notebook entry: "On visiting Texas—something is missing: it's Europe, it's the world missing."

As was the case with certain other women writers from these parts, most notably Katherine Anne Porter and Gertrude Beasley, Texas was not nearly big enough, culturally, to contain Highsmith's aspirations and talents. She sought a national and international audience, and she found one. Sometimes Texas treats its women writers better after they are dead, especially the ones who went away. Three of the fiercest women writers you can think of, Katherine Anne Porter, Gertrude Beasley, and Patricia Highsmith, all had their beginnings in Texas, and they all left Texas in pursuit of their art.

2004

In Joan Schenkar's new biography, *The Talented Miss Highsmith* (2009), an even darker portrait of the author emerges. Schenkar's book is loaded with steamy details about Highsmith's raging libido, her penchant for seducing married women of wealth and privilege, and her perverse and murderous imagination. Perhaps my favorite example of her tendencies is a list—she was a compulsive list-maker—titled "Little Crimes for Little Tots." She enumerated eight ways that tots could murder their parents using simple household tools and chemicals found lying about in any middle-class dwelling.

The Texas context receives new emphasis as well. One editor declared her to be "Texas tough." And there is this detail: at one point the University of Texas offered her $25,000 for her manuscripts, letters, etc., to which Highsmith scoffed that the offer was insulting, nothing more than the price of a used car.

GIANT

Lyndon Johnson's johnson was called Jumbo. He named it that himself early in life, when he was a mere college lad in San Marcos. LBJ was always proud of Jumbo. Like Walt Whitman, he might have said, "There is that lot of me, and all so luscious." He was also unselfish with other bodily functions. In the full flush of his egotism, a toilet for LBJ was just another seat of power.

The Jumbo revelations are part of the intimate portrait of LBJ by Robert Caro in the third installment of his magnum opus, *The Years of Lyndon Johnson,* which was launched in 1982. The latest, subtitled *Master of the Senate* (the sobriquet is borrowed from that old phrase-maker Doris Kearns Goodwin), weighs in at a whopping 1,040 pages of text, with an additional 141 pages of sources and notes. And the new volume covers only twelve years, from Landslide Lyndon's ascension to the Senate in 1949 to his departure in 1960 to serve as Jack Kennedy's vice president. These books, like presidential libraries, are getting out of hand. Think of it: Caro has ahead of him the 1960 presidential campaign; LBJ's sulky and fretful years as V.P., when he played cattle lot to the Kennedys' Camelot; the assassination; LBJ's ascendance to the presidency; the Great Society; Vietnam; the decision not to run in 1968; and the retirement years at the ranch in Johnson City. Do the math: we're looking at 4,000–5,000 pages minimum.

There are other biographers of LBJ of course, but Caro still does the best job of creating a word picture of Johnson's physicality and his difficult personality. Often it isn't pretty. Johnson devoted his whole life to attaining power, and to further his progress along the "path to power" (the author's recurrent metaphor for Johnson's life), he would, in Caro's words, "let nothing stand in his way."

Power, it seemed, always resided in older men, often lonely older men, and Johnson played the role of "professional son" to a degree that disgusted many of his contemporaries. His M.O. was always the same: to identify the most important person in any organization in which he found himself and then ingratiate himself to that person. After a session with an elderly senator, Johnson told John Connally, "Christ, I've been kissing asses all my life." In the House of Representatives the object of his affection was the Speaker of the House, Sam Rayburn, and in his case, it was the Speaker's bald dome that Johnson kissed. He told uncounted numbers of older, influential men that they were like a "daddy" to him, and each lapped it up.

In the Senate Johnson's rapid rise to the top derived from his courtship of Richard Russell, of Georgia, another lonely bachelor. A subtext of Caro's book is the degree to which flattery plays a role in the lives of successful public figures. No Renaissance courtier ever wooed a king or a queen more ardently than Lyndon Johnson wooed those who stood in a position to help him. Yet it must be said that Johnson had much to offer. There are toadies who are nauseatingly adept at flattery and whose abilities stop there, but Johnson impressed all the lonely, powerful men with his brains and charm, his political astuteness that rose to the level of genius, and his burning ambition.

Along with Johnson's capacity to win influential friends, however, Caro reveals his willingness to be ruthless when it suited his goals. The example of Leland Olds is an instructive one. Now forgotten, Olds was the chairman of the Federal Power Commission and a longtime champion of the rights of the common man against the interests of power companies. In Johnson's heroic fight to bring electrification to rural Hill Country Texans in the thirties, he was allied with Leland Olds. But in 1949, when Johnson saw an opportunity to do something for his oil-and-gas-rich backers in Texas, Olds, who favored regulating the price of natural gas, became a target. Johnson's subcommittee hearings on Olds's reappointment to the power commission turned into a commie smear job orchestrated by Johnson. During a break in the hearings, before Olds was turned down for reappointment and his life essentially ruined, the junior senator from Texas told him, "I hope you understand there's nothing personal in this. . . . It's only politics, you know."

But of course that was just bull, because it *was* personal. For Lyndon Johnson the personal and the political were one and the same. Sometimes Johnson's need for power required him to do bad things, and he did them. But sometimes a national good fell into alignment with his overweening ambition, and in those instances he shone.

The greatest of these moments—before Johnson assumed the presidency—occurred in 1956, when his desire to hold the highest office in the land coincided with the pressure building for a civil rights bill. If Johnson was ever to ascend to the presidency, he had to escape the taint of being a sectional candidate; he had to cleanse himself of the odor of magnolias. Before this time, Johnson had been ideologically as lily-white as any son of the South one could name. His first major Senate speech began, "We of the South," and many of his fat-cat supporters and political operatives were racist to the core. LBJ could use the n-word with the best of them, though as in other areas, he usually adjusted his rhetoric to fit his audience. He was so successful at camouflaging his feelings on issues that he always fooled both conservatives and liberals into believing he was on their side. But there was always just one side: his own.

For decades the Southern bloc, led by Johnson's carefully cultivated friend Richard Russell, had successfully thwarted all efforts by Northern liberals to pass anything that would alleviate the inequities and injustices of Jim Crow–ism in the eleven former Confederate states, of which Texas, of course, was one. But in 1957 Johnson crafted a compromise that would simultaneously lead to the passage of the first civil rights bill since Reconstruction and set the stage for his presidential campaign in

1960. Caro is eloquent on the moral necessity of a civil rights bill, devoting six chapters, almost two hundred pages, to the legislative genius displayed by Johnson in getting a bill passed. Even if the bill that was finally passed was only "a crumb," as Hubert Humphrey said, at least it offered hope for the future, a promissory note that LBJ would himself redeem during the finest hours of his presidency, the passage of the 1964 and 1965 Civil Rights Acts.

Perhaps policy wonks will find all of the insider details about the Byzantine workings of the Senate as interesting and necessary as Caro seems to think they are, but for some readers, the first hundred pages, in effect a history of the Senate, make for a mighty slow start before Lyndon Johnson comes striding onto the scene. And some of the chapters add little to our understanding of the man we already know almost too much about. We know, for example, that he will do everything necessary to win, at whatever cost to his health or that of his subordinates, and we know that his buddies in Texas will deliver all the money he needs, when he needs it. Johnson liked greenbacks, and his devoted cronies, many of them movers and shakers in the Lone Star State, took envelopes and grocery sacks stuffed with cash on their trips to D.C.; they dared not leave home without it.

A New Yorker, Caro struggles manfully to get details about the sunny Southland right, but sometimes he stumbles. He says, for example, that one of LBJ's favorite colorful expressions was to describe a hard rain as being like "a cat pissing on a flat rock," when the saying, hardly unique to LBJ, refers to a cow, not a cat. Caro also seems to believe that the word "Nigra" was used by Alabamians as a synonym for the double-*g* word.

In the end, Caro is unable to plumb the depths of LBJ's driven personality. He keeps going back to the childhood humiliations suffered by the boy Lyndon when his father experienced irreversible economic setbacks and to the grinding physical labor that Lyndon performed working on the hardscrabble land of the Texas Hill Country. Still, none of these factors explains why Johnson, in many of his personal dealings—with his wife, with his staff, with strangers, with anybody who irritated him or didn't jump when he said "frog"—treated people so cruelly. Plenty of poor boys who became rich and successful, and whose upbringing was as hard as his, continued to deal decently with people. Not Johnson. He was a towering, often insufferable man, and yet he accomplished some great things, and to many of those who knew him, he possessed enormous personal charm and magnetism.

If Johnson's defining passion was the pursuit of power, Caro's is the pursuit of Johnson himself. I look forward, I guess, to seeing what Caro digs up about LBJ that we don't already know. I would be very interested, for example, in seeing Caro's take on Lyndon Johnson's conversations with Jackie Kennedy just weeks after her husband's death. These exchanges are on tape and have been published, and they also appear in an interesting recent novel, Adam Braver's *November 22, 1963,* published in 2008. Braver quotes the key bits in his novel. In a phone call on December 2, less than two weeks after the assassination, the President called Jackie "sweetie" and flirtatiously invited her to visit him at the White House. On December 7 he told her that she looked "gorgeous" in a recent photograph and again implored her to visit the White House so they could take a walk "down to the seesaw . . . like old times." The last thing he told her was to hug her children and "tell them I'd like to be their daddy." It appears that Jumbo had become Daddy, but he was still the same old Jumbo.

2002

LBJ's larger-than-life displays knew few bounds. There is the oft-reported incident in a White House meeting with the Secretary of State and others in attendance, when Johnson unzipped his pants and displayed the size of his member compared to what he imagined Ho Chi Mihn's might be. In the end, however, the little guy would prevail over the big guy.

Speaking of pants, a recently released tape from the LBJ Library, titled "President Johnson orders pants from Joe Haggar," has become an instant classic on YouTube. On the phone to the clothier Joe Haggar, Johnson goes into great detail describing how he wants his pants tailored. Here is the most salient moment: "And another thing—the crotch, down where your nuts hang—is always a little too tight, so when you make them up, give me an inch that I can let out there, uh because they cut me, it's just like riding a wire fence."

THE WRITE BROTHERS

In *Donald Barthelme: The Genesis of a Cool Sound* (Texas A&M University Press), Helen Moore Barthelme, the writer's second wife, recalls her life with the man she considered a "literary genius." Perhaps he was. He certainly thought so, and in the sixties he had a huge impact on the American literary scene. John Barth called him the "thinking man's minimalist." Another admirer, Thomas Pynchon, referred to Barthelme's world as "Barthelmismo."

Barthelme possessed an imperial assurance about his writing. When an editor at the *New Yorker* said ten lines needed to be cut from a story that used the word "butter" 132 times, Barthelme replied that "the word butter must appear 132 times, you can cut out any other butter after that." The story in question, "Eugénie Grandet," was collected in *Sixty Stories,* Barthelme's own selection of his best. Looking at it today, it's hard to see how a paragraph consisting entirely of the word "butter" repeated 86 times makes much difference at all.

The jury is still out on the magnitude of Barthelme's accomplishment. The downside of his brand of surrealism or metafiction or postmodernism or whatever you choose to call it is that it is often tied to ephemeral pop culture references, and what can seem hip and cool in one decade can later seem precious and irrelevant. The more experimental stories, for example, were print equivalents of collage—fragmented combinations of photographs, cartoons, bold headlines, quotations, and often the merest hint of a narrative line, or none at all. The more conventional stories, such as the hilarious "The School," a dead-on satire of politically correct thinking by a trendy teacher, seem to hold up better today.

Still, there are many pleasures to be found in such avant-garde exercises as "Brain Damage," in which, for instance, an out-of-nowhere anthropological riff on a people called the Wapituil produces very funny moments. The Wapituil "have everything that we have, but only one of each thing." As a result, "they have one disease, mononucleosis" and "the sex life of a Wapituil consists of a single experience, which he thinks about for a long time." Whether the with-it-ness of the culture-bound stories will last is an open question. For example, the annual *MLA International Bibliography,* the Dun and Bradstreet of academic approbation, listed 11 articles on Barthelme for 1997 and 1998 and 230 on Toni Morrison for the same period.

Reading Barthelme's stories, one would deduce an education at a good East Coast school and an upbringing in a suitably fashionable Manhattan apartment. The facts could not be more different. Although born in Philadelphia in 1931, he grew up in the provinces, in barbaric Texas, in the thirties and forties. But here is another surprise for the stereotypically inclined. One of the side benefits of Helen Barthelme's book is its portrait of how sophisticated Houston was in the fifties; the city boasted lively scenes in painting, music, and drama.

Culture started at home, and it started early in the Barthelme family. For Barthelme's fourteenth birthday, his father gave him a copy of Marcel Raymond's *From Baudelaire to Surrealism.* Barthelme went to the University of Houston, not Princeton or Harvard or even Rice, and he read *Waiting for Godot* in Houston too, a work that gave him a perfect absurdist model for the kind of new fiction he wanted to write.

In Helen Barthelme's re-creation of his life, her husband was always seeking—but never getting—his father's approval. The son rebelled early on, running off to Mexico when he was sixteen. After high school he played drums in a band against his father's wishes. As an adult, he ended up arguing with

Donald Senior over one thing or another at nearly every family get-together.

The father loomed large in his son's consciousness, so omnipresent that one of Barthelme's novels was called *The Dead Father,* in which he brooded, postmodernly, on everything from the father's penis to the size of the son's responsibility as inheritor of fatherness: "You must become your father, but a paler, weaker version of him." Donald Senior, an architect of some local standing, helped design the rather grand Hall of State at Fair Park in Dallas, built for the Texas Centennial. Barthelme the son designed stories with graphic elements and bits of ornamentation. The mother, Helen Bechtold Barthelme, was equally brilliant in her own fashion. Everybody in the Barthelme family was brilliant, it seems. Recalls Helen Moore Barthelme: "Each Barthelme had a different kind of humor, but all were unique, and I have never known anyone else like them."

Whatever market value Barthelme's literary stock eventually levels out at, the sheer literary talent and output of the Barthelme family has never, I think, been sufficiently recognized. Perhaps only the James family—Henry, William, Henry Senior—surpasses them in this regard. Besides Donald's career (eight short-story collections, four novels, a children's book, an illustrated narrative, and an international reputation), the other four children—Joan, Peter, Frederick (Rick), and Steven—have had remarkable careers as well. Joan became the first female executive at Pennzoil in a male-dominated Houston corporate world. Peter, a successful advertising executive, has published three witty, hard-boiled crime novels set in Houston and the Gulf Coast. Frederick's career is amazing. After a precocious beginning as a minimalist artist, he became one of the foremost exponents of minimalism in fiction, though his more recent work represents an exfoliation of experience that goes beyond the sometimes tiresome limitations of minimalism. In twelve volumes of fiction, including several books of short stories and novels such as *Bob the Gambler* and *The Brothers,* he has become the premier chronicler of Mississippi Gulf Coast suburban culture. The youngest of the Barthelmes, Steven, has published a collection of short fiction and coauthored, with Frederick, the compelling memoir of their descent into gambling hell, *Double Down: Reflections on Gambling and Loss.*

Perhaps the key to Donald's family romance resides in the book by his two younger brothers. Their description of their parents suggests a hard act to follow: "He and Mother made of the family and our early lives a lovely old-fashioned movie with snappy dialogue and surprising developments, high drama and low comedy, heroes and villains, wit and beauty and regret. Pretty much everything since then has been anticlimax."

In his own life Donald tried to achieve perfection. That was all he expected of his marriage to Helen: perfection. They had to have the right house, the right furniture, the right books, the right everything. And all of this cost money, which Barthelme did not have—never would. He depended on Helen, whose advertising business was profitable, and, painfully, on his father. He wanted to live as an elite without paying the freight. Helen calls him "autocratic" rather than "arrogant."

Perfectionists are rarely satisfied with the way things turn out in real life, and Barthelme certainly found imperfection everywhere he looked. He might have looked more closely at himself. Though he had jettisoned Catholicism (as did all the brothers; that was one vaccination that didn't take), he spoke often to Helen of "this evil world."

Ditching Helen the way he did was one of his less-perfect acts. In 1962 he moved to New York, the locus of all his artistic desire, and while there, waiting for Helen to join him, he found he liked it without her. New York gave him access to movers and shakers like the artist Elaine de Kooning, the critic Dwight Macdonald, and many other luminaries in the arts who were thrilling to be around. The in-crowd in New York drank a great deal, and Barthelme, in Helen's words, began "drinking excessively."

Eventually he and Helen decided to separate, and while he was in Denmark on a Guggenheim, he took up with a Scandinavian beauty named Birgit who suffered from a debilitating inherited disease and mental problems. When she became pregnant, Barthelme insisted upon divorcing Helen to keep the child from being illegitimate. Helen is reserved in her account of that particular bloodletting done from afar, but she does report that when his novel *Snow White* came out in 1967, she ripped out the dedication to Birgit.

In the early eighties Barthelme returned to Texas and assumed the mantle of éminence grise in creative writing at the University of Houston. His life was cut short in 1989 by cancer. After he was cremated, Frederick, in a gesture Donald would have appreciated, Helen says, poked around in the ashes in his fireplace, wondering aloud where Donald was. When the parents died in quick succession in the nineties, Frederick and Steven lost their inheritance in a frenzy of high-stakes games in the offshore casinos along the Mississippi coast. Such self-inflicted suffering seems to have deepened and extended their writing, but the most famous of the Barthelmes had always relied on irony to mask the messiness of daily existence. One of the virtues, and sadnesses, of Helen Barthelme's arresting account is its revelation of just how melancholy the life behind the polished surfaces of Donald's stories actually was.

2001

Helen Barthelme, who died in 2002, was a classmate of mine in graduate school at the University of Texas in the late 1960s. She was a delightful woman who threw elegant parties. She told me once that I reminded her of Donald Barthelme, of his sense of humor. Perhaps so, but Donald apparently did not think I was very funny. In 1986, in an article for *Texas Monthly,* Barthelme took out after me for something I had written about Texas writers falling into two camps: the Redskins and the Palefaces. He objected mightily to my denigration of "fern bar writers." Here is what he wrote: "Did he mean faggot homosexual queer pansy fairies? And if so, why didn't he say so?" But all I was talking about was new writers coming into the state and becoming, overnight, "Texas" writers. To my mind "fern bar" was descriptive, not a code word for something else. All that mattered in the end was the quality of the writing. For anyone who might be interested in the little literary skirmishes that took place in Texas in the 1980s, there is an excellent compendium of all points of view in *Range Wars: Heated Debates, Sober Reflections, and Other Assessments of Texas Writing,* edited by Craig Clifford and Tom Pilkington (SMU, 1989).

In 2009 Tracy Daugherty, a former student and friend of Barthelme's at the University of Houston, published a well-written, richly detailed biography of the writer titled *Hiding Man: A Biography of Donald Barthelme.* Daugherty makes the strongest case to date for Barthelme's continuing importance in American letters.

EXPATRIATE ACT

Of all contemporary Texas writers, no one shines brighter in the pantheon of Lone Star lit than John Graves. Why this should be so is less a matter of critical exegesis than one of conviction, of belief. The reputation, the legend, the legacy, all derive from one book, *Goodbye to a River,* published in 1960 and continuously in print ever since. The work arrived at a propitious moment in Texas letters; the old guard of Dobie, Webb, and Bedichek was about to fade from the scene, and Graves's narrative about a canoe trip down a stretch of the Brazos River seemed to mark both the summation and the end of something: the land-centered ethic of Old Texas. In this one book, Graves combined Webb's interest in history, Bedichek's in nature, and Dobie's in folklore into a seamless whole that was greater, and more literary, than any single work by any one of the celebrated triumvirate.

Readers responded to *Goodbye to a River* on several levels. They liked its elegiac tone. They liked the avuncular wisdom that Graves sought to impart. They liked the book's muted ecological thrust (Graves is no bomb-thrower, no Edward Abbey). Graves's ruminative manner conveyed a sense of validation to Texans with a strong and often sentimental attachment to the land, whether they were "old farts" (a favorite Graves term) who owned a few acres and liked to putter around on them, absentee owners who romanticized how wonderful it was on a farm or ranch when they were growing up, or the folks, mostly male, who liked to hunt and fish. The book was also just literary enough, stuffed as it is with allusions to Shakespeare, Shelley, Yeats, Thoreau, and Hemingway, to make readers feel that they were getting a dose of culture along with their wing shots and string of crappie.

Graves was forty when *Goodbye to a River* came out, and before it there had been a long foreground of false starts in fiction, most of which grew out of his experiences in Europe in the fifties, before he discovered his true subject, hardscrabble Texas. Katherine Anne Porter, Gertrude Beasley, William Humphrey, and William Goyen each lived in Europe for a time, and they all wrote their best work about a remembered Texas past. Graves's process of artistic discovery took a different path, however, as he demonstrates in his newest offering, *Myself and Strangers: A Memoir of Apprenticeship* (Alfred A. Knopf, 2004). It is a backward glance at his life, from his middle-class upbringing in Fort Worth (his father was a clothing merchant) through a two-and-a-half-year period spent abroad searching, he says, for himself and for his voice. Although he seems to have found himself in Europe, he did not find his voice until he came home to Texas, where he embraced a deeply rooted provincialism—the stony ground and Southwestern ethos of the small landholder—that has formed the basis of his best work.

Before getting to the expatriate years, the book touches on Graves's education at Rice University; his service in the Marine Corps during World War II (he was blinded in one eye on Saipan); nine months spent in Mexico sharpening his Spanish; more education, at Columbia University; a four-year marriage; and even a brief stint teaching freshman English at the University of Texas. His description of that soul-destroying labor helps explain the desire to travel: "A basically miserable, overworked, underpaid period, teaching indifferent freshmen and walking around full of guilt about the ungraded themes sticking out of my coat pockets. I was getting no writing done, nor was our marriage in the best of shape."

The book moves through this material rapidly and then

lingers—for too long, some readers will think—on the years in Spain, with side trips to London and Paris; it concentrates on "the time between the autumns of 1951 and 1956," which included the key years of his experience abroad. Famous expatriate memoirs like Hemingway's *A Moveable Feast* are accessible to us because of the company the author kept. Hemingway met everybody, and everybody he met was important: Stein, Picasso, Fitzgerald, Dos Passos, Joyce—almost the entire roll call of modernism. Most memoirs of Paris in the twenties have the same cast of great characters, people who profoundly mattered because they were defining the twentieth century in painting, sculpture, and literature.

But the people Graves met in the fifties were, by and large, nobodies. He says so himself, describing one group of "fellow countrymen" as "aimless, upper class, usually charming, heavy drinkers. They are really nobodies." Not that there weren't great figures to be glimpsed from a distance. The distance was self-imposed; Graves could have met them, but something in him kept him from doing so. In the case of Hemingway, his reticence is understandable. Once, in Pamplona in 1953, he observed Hemingway at a table, surrounded by admirers. Papa was having a drink and demonstrating how to handle a bullfighting cape, but Graves felt that the celebrated author had probably become someone who would disappoint him. Graves was under the spell of Hemingway's early work—what American writer who went to Spain in 1953 was not?

On Mallorca, that island of "hard-drinking idlers" where Graves lingered fretfully for most of a year, he could have met a great writer who lived there and bore the same last name. Robert Graves, the British poet, novelist, and memoirist, had written a stellar autobiography, *Goodbye to All That,* whose success had enabled him to leave England and take up residence on Mallorca. But the book of Robert's that John admired was *The White Goddess,* a study of the essential role of the female consciousness as muse and inspiration. (Everybody admired it; Sylvia Plath and Ted Hughes virtually used it as a marriage manual.) Yet the

American Graves never tried to make contact with the English Graves.

Eventually Graves grew so tired of the wastrel Americans on Mallorca that he wrote a highly critical sketch about them that was published in *Holiday* magazine. It was the only thing he ever wrote in anger, he says, and he felt bad about it. Some of those who recognized themselves in the article never forgave him (and he has not seen fit in the years since to reprint the piece). During all this time in Europe, Graves was trying to write. He wrote two types of stories: "one for them and one for me" — "them" being the slick magazines that paid well, the "one for me" being the literary stuff that was slower to sell (and write) and earned little or no money. Graves would eventually concentrate all his efforts on the literary side, but even then he felt a lack. He needed a book; only that would provide the "status" he required. This is one of the recurrent themes in the journal that Graves kept during his years abroad. "Time is moving along and I am farting around, writing halfassedly on insignificant stuff," he berates himself in December 1953, and then, the next month: "A book, a book, a book is what I need to write."

The book he pinned his hopes on back then never happened. He worked on a novel called "A Speckled Horse" in 1955 and 1956 while living in Spain and then in Sag Harbor, New York, but his agent didn't like it. Graves thinks the book was "quite masculine" for his agent's sensibility, which he describes as "gentle, civilized, and effete," but on the basis of the segment he chose to reprint in *A John Graves Reader,* the agent seems to have been right. The prose sometimes sounds like an entry in the "bad Hemingway" contest: "Without his willing it Hill's eyes flicked down the length of her body and back up again to her face momentarily, and something moved far down inside him. It had been a long time. He knew that she knew the thing had moved inside of him, and knew that she liked that."

The memoir bogs down when Graves quotes verbatim from his journal, which he does fairly frequently. One entry from August 5, 1953, is typical: "Pepe's troubles. Had supper with him this evening, and after he had told me his worries we had good

talk about a little of everything. I like him better and better."
Pepe is José Mut, a friend notable for nothing else to command
our attention. And then there are the women. Graves describes
a "purgative, jolly, and guiltless romp" with one Spanish woman
and a prolonged affair with a French beauty "who was very good
in bed." So it goes in the easy latitudes of desire.

To be successful, journal entries have to be about famous
people or be written with the burning intensity of deep anguish,
like, say, those of Sylvia Plath. At times Graves's entries are flat,
like the ones all of us write when we travel: "Sitting in the bar
Bellver at 10:30 a.m., waiting for your *café con leche* and crois-
sants, checking the comically moral front page of the newspaper
Baleares . . ." At some level he knows that his reliance on old material and obscure actors in a personal drama from fifty years ago
is a problem, and so he calls upon "Old John" to comment on
what "Young John" was up to, but it's not enough to overcome
the datedness of the diary.

Yet there are quite a few moments of insight too. He describes, for example, the pleasure of reading John Houghton
Allen's *Southwest,* a book from Graves's homeland published in
1952. It was a reminder that it might be possible to write about
Texas, that perhaps the true places of the heart could be found
there rather than in foreign climes.

By the fall of 1955 Graves had returned stateside, and by the
"drouth-breaking autumn of 1957," he was on the Brazos River,
storing up images and experiences. The book that resulted was,
he writes in his memoir, a "liberation" from the self-doubt of the
years in Spain. With this act of personal repatriation, Graves had
come full circle.

In retrospect, his career seems to mark the end of a certain
tradition in Texas letters favoring essays and sketches about the
natural world. Stephen Harrigan has moved away from such
nonfiction to write novels and screenplays; Rick Bass has been so
long in Montana that he rarely writes of Texas anymore; and I
can't think of anyone else following the Bedichek-Graves trail.

The fact that Texas is overwhelmingly urban breeds less and
less connection with the land. Still, Texans harry the corn-fed

deer for trophy antlers, tee it up and feel close to God, go tubing in loud groups down the Guadalupe—all activities of the kind that Graves deplores in *Goodbye to a River* as "the climactic ejaculation of city tensions." Nature lovers have always been hard on those of us in cities pent.

2004

NATION STATE

Springtime in Texas is different than it is in other places; here we have to rave about the goddam blue-bonnets and remember the Alamo and a whole bunch of other stuff: Texas Independence Day, Goliad, San Jacinto. I can hear the speeches now. Every year it's the same thing, and every year I forget which day is Independence Day until I hear the cannons roar on the UT campus.

But what I want to know is, does anybody care about our past? The landscape of the long ago is still meaningful to members of the Texas State Historical Association, historians, and those lonely readers who frequent the Texana sections of bookstores, but what about the rest of Texas? And the country at large? For those who have recently arrived here, Travis is the name of a county, and Austin and Houston are the names of cities (and universities). For those who have never set foot in the state, the Alamo is probably the only historical name they associate with the state, outside of presidents LBJ and Bush I and Bush II.

Is there a national constituency for Texas history? Two recent books by well-established historians bring up the question anew by the very fact of their publication: H. W. Brands's *Lone Star Nation: How a Ragged Army of Volunteers Won the Battle for Texas Independence—and Changed America* and William C. Davis's *Lone Star Rising: The Revolutionary Birth of the Texas Republic*. Both titles, cut from the same license plate logo, echo the most widely read history of the state in modern times, T. R. Fehrenbach's *Lone Star:*

A History of Texas and the Texans (1968). The titles also seek to link Texas with national issues, and both were published by prestigious trade presses: Doubleday and Free Press, respectively. Neither author hails from Texas. Brands, who lives in Austin and teaches at the University of Texas, grew up in Oregon; and Davis, from Missouri, is the director of programs at Virginia Tech's Center for Civil War Studies. Both are extremely prolific. Brands has specialized in books on iconic Americans, having written biographies of Benjamin Franklin, Dwight Eisenhower, Woodrow Wilson, Theodore Roosevelt, and FDR, among others. He has also written books on U.S. foreign policy, the Cold War, and the California gold rush. You name it, Brands has branded it. Davis is no slouch in the productivity department either. He has written or edited some forty-odd volumes on the Civil War and the history of the South.

So why did these two historians, with track records of publishing books on topics of great moment to the nation, turn to Texas? In a promotional appearance at BookPeople, in Austin, Davis said he had grown tired of writing about the Civil War. This is not his first foray into these parts, however. His well-regarded *Three Roads to the Alamo: The Lives and Fortunes of David Crockett, James Bowie, and William Barret Travis* won a Texas Institute of Letters prize in 1999. Brands, having lived in Texas for over twenty years, seems naturally to have gravitated toward Texas as a subject; in 2003 he wrote a provocative article for *Texas Monthly* arguing that the defense of the Alamo was a military mistake.

Curiously, both books begin with a brief history of the arrival of sediment in Texas. Sediment, which is a fancy word for dirt, is not a subject likely to hold a reader's attention for long, and so each author quickly moves to topics of greater interest.

Both of them, but especially Davis, spend a lot of time on the minor uprisings, revolts, and attempts by adventurers and freebooters to seize Texas from Spain, then from Mexico, before the final cataclysmic events of 1835 and 1836. Most were small-time operations, but there was one rebellion rather stunning in its magnitude. On August 18, 1813, about twenty miles south of San

Antonio, rebel forces numbering approximately 1,400 and composed of Americans, Tejanos, and various Indians clashed with a large Spanish royalist army led by General Joaquín de Arredondo. More than 1,000 of the rebels were killed, and Arredondo set a bloody precedent for dealing with insurrectionists in the distant province of Texas by ordering the summary execution of those captured. Does any of this sound familiar? Not to me. The Battle of Medina, the largest and bloodiest ever fought on Texas soil, is one we missed in my Texas history class. Among Arredondo's subalterns, incidentally, was a nineteen-year-old lieutenant named Santa Anna.

While Davis expends many pages on the long foreground, Brands pursues another tack. He creates a stronger narrative line by following first one figure for a few pages, then another, to drive the story along. Some of them, like Noah Smithwick—who authored a rousing autobiography, *The Evolution of a State, or Recollections of Old Texas Days* (1900)—are well known, at least among Texas history buffs. But others, such as W. B. Dewees, are quite obscure. An early settler, one of Stephen F. Austin's "Three Hundred," Dewees later published a memoir, *Letters from an Early Settler of Texas* (1852), whose authenticity has been challenged by other historians (as Brands notes in his bibliography).

Another little-known figure that Brands uses to especially good effect is the melancholy general Manuel de Mier y Terán. Sent north by the Mexican government to observe the activities of the American settlers who had moved into Texas, Terán in 1828 saw much that was admirable and much that was disturbing. The Americans were thriving, and they followed their instincts for land and profit. Terán concluded that American avidity needed to be curbed or else the province would be lost. He suggested sending more troops to Texas and putting an end to further settlement. Back in Mexico, Terán watched with mistrust as Santa Anna seized power in 1832 and Texas grew more rebellious. To a friend he said, "We are lost. Texas is lost." It was all too much for him, and so he literally fell on his own sword.

Brands, whose narrative skills are impressive, brings William B. Travis vividly to life by quoting juicily from Travis's

journal: "*Chingaba una mujer que es cincuenta y seis en mi vida.*"
Translation: "I ****ed a woman that is the fifty-sixth in my life."
"Chingada," spelled quaintly by Travis, is an essential word in
schoolyards round the state.

After reading the two books back-to-back, I was still puzzled
as to whether Texas's early history will have resonance outside
the state — or in it, for that matter. So I asked Brands why he
thought the Texas story would appeal to the rest of the country.
"The Alamo," he said simply. "There's something about the story
of the Alamo, of what happens to people when they know they
are going to die."

He has a point. I came away from both books feeling as
though all of the preliminary buildup had been a long prelude
to the Alamo chapters. Most of the schemers and dreamers of
a Texas empire-to-be wound up at the Alamo. It ennobled the
trinity of Travis, Bowie, and Crockett, redeeming their lives
from disorder, busted plans, and careers on the near side of ab-
ject failure. But neither Brands nor Davis brings much that is
new to the Alamo story. Had Thomas Ricks Lindley's *Alamo
Traces: New Evidence and New Conclusions* (Republic of Texas Press,
2003) been available when they were writing, the Alamo chapters might have been more interesting. Lindley argues, for example, that Crockett left the Alamo on March 3, traveled to
Gonzales, and returned on March 4, just two days before the
end, with 53 new reinforcements. This bit of heroic recruiting
boosts the role of Crockett at the Alamo, increases the number
of defenders to approximately 250, and casts further aspersions
on those who did not come to the aid of Travis and his besieged
men.

The most prominent Texan who was not at the Alamo was
Sam Houston, and Brands and Davis both do a good job of trying to plumb this most inconsistent, wily, and inscrutable figure
(almost any virtue that can be attributed to him can be counter-
balanced by a vice of equal gravity). Many of Houston's actions
from just before the Battle of the Alamo to several days afterward simply cannot be explained. Even his decisive victory at
San Jacinto is shrouded in uncertainty. The fateful decision to

turn right at a forked road, toward the swampy grasslands of San Jacinto, instead of left toward Nacogdoches and further retreat — even that action, so crucial to subsequent events, cannot be explained. We still don't know whether it was Houston's decision or one forced upon him by his democratic army.

When I was growing up, Texas history was a lot easier to follow. Travis drew a line in the sediment. Crockett went down swinging. Bowie dispatched many Mexicans from his sickbed. Moses Rose chose not to stay, swung over the wall, then morphed, later on, into Glenn Ford in *The Man From the Alamo.* And nobody told us Sam Houston was a big drunk. Besides, anything important that we wanted to know could be found in that delectable comic book with the curious title, *Texas History Movies.* This publication, which first appeared in a large-format book in 1928, was widely circulated throughout schools in the state. It made Texas history fun. At one time most seventh-graders in the state read this book if they read nothing else. Looking back at it today, one is struck by the vigor and liveliness of the cartoon panels and the language of the captions. In one, for example, an angry Spanish governor kicks a black cat, exclaiming, "Caramba, Bring that scoundrel to me. I'll fix him." But it's the larger caption describing the action that surprises me today: THE GOVERNOR WAXED EXCEEDINGLY WROTHFUL. Now that's language. But proponents of political correctness eventually censored *Texas History Movies.* In 1974 the Texas State Historical Association put together a sensitive panel to consider the panels, and the result was an expurgated edition. The black cat, for example, was removed from the picture. Too violent, one supposes. But children love seeing violence depicted, or they used to anyway. The great offender was not black cats, of course, but racial stereotyping of Indians (Native Americans), blacks (African Americans), and Mexicans (Mexican Americans). All of the stereotyping was excised or altered. Reading the original panels, we never stopped to think.

Now we are asked to *think* about everything. It can be tiresome. Both books dramatize two big-picture themes. The first is that the spirit of democracy formed a tide in the affairs of Texans that could not be stemmed, not by politicians, generals, massacres, or anything else. The other is that the Texas Revolution mirrors the American Revolution. The little cannon that fired at Mexican troops at Gonzales on October 2, 1835, is our Lexington, our Concord, the shot heard round Coahuila y Texas; the Texas Declaration of Independence is a derivative and less eloquent version of the Philadelphia document; and so on. In any case, the Texas Revolution was certainly shorter and more compact. Instead of stretching over eight long years like the American Revolution, its duration was one month less than that of a full-term pregnancy, and it produced only three events for students to memorize: the fall of the Alamo, on March 6, 1836; the execution of Colonel James W. Fannin's troops at Goliad shortly thereafter; and finally, the decisive eighteen-minute battle of San Jacinto, on April 21. Oh yes, and Texas Independence Day, which I think is on March 2.

I don't know what the sales figures for these two books were, but I do know what the ticket sales were for *The Alamo,* Hollywood's most recent attempt to sell Texas history to the nation. They were miserable. Released in May 2004 at an estimated cost of $120 million, this expensive, amateurish, tedious film earned a grand total of $22 million by year's end. In comparison, *Shrek 2* raked in $437 million and *Spider-Man 2* $373 million. (Perhaps they should have called it *Alamo 2.*) Another film about sacrifice, *The Passion of the Christ,* made $370 million. Even compared with other bad historical epics released that year, *The Alamo* fared badly. *Troy,* riding mainly on the strength of Brad Pitt's buffed body, earned $113 million, and Oliver Stone's much maligned *Alexander* managed to out-earn *The Alamo* by $12 million. What went wrong? Just about everything. Leonard Maltin, a familiar name in popular film criticism, said it best. He considered the project doomed from the start: "The younger demographic already doesn't like the Western. It has no interest in history, especially American history. Today's moviegoers don't care about the Alamo." I couldn't have said it better myself. One mistake of local interest, in my view, is that they relied too much on the advice of academic Texas historians obsessed with historical accuracy. The results were pointless. The film went to such lengths as getting the buttons on the Mexican Army's uniforms exactly correct according to the historical record, and embedded Texas historians were on hand to see to it that the correct flags were always flying in the correct scenes. The filmmakers even hired a professor of Spanish and Portuguese to make sure that the caste system of spoken Spanish was represented in the film. More marinated in Texas history than any Alamo movie, it was also more boring. They would have made a better movie if they'd just filmed the comic book *Texas History Movies*.

2004

The ubiquity of the Lone Star in Texas is rather amazing. In Austin alone, presumably the least Texan of all cities because of its elitist blue-state standing, it's possible to do just about everything under the sign of the Lone Star. You can have Lone Star Doughnuts for breakfast, a Lone Star Sub for lunch, a Lone Star beer for breakfast or lunch or both; you can keep your dinero at a Lone Star Bank, take Lone Star Bee Pollen to combat allergies, get cash for stuff at Lone Star Pawns, swank around town in a Lone Star Limo, stash your swag in a Lone Star Self-Storage, take your pet to a Lone Star Veterinarian, seek enlightenment at Lone Star Points of Knowledge, get your leaks fixed by Lone Star Plumbing, practice your putting on a Lone Star Putting Green, have your cancer monitored at Lone Star Oncology, and when that great Lone Star trumpet in the sky calls you home, you can go out in style at the Lone Star Hospice. It's not quite cradle to grave, but it's damned close.

ALL THE
PRETTY CORPSES

A new novel by Cormac McCarthy is always an event, and in the case of *No Country for Old Men,* the author's first outing since he finished the Border Trilogy, the cormacmccarthy.com Web site was so excited they counted down the minutes: the day my copy arrived the clock showed 109 days, 15 hours, 17 minutes, and 42.41.40 seconds to the publication date. (The Web site was created in 1995 by the Cormac McCarthy Society—a loose confederation of enthusiasts, academics, and the curious who pore over Cormackian lore with the zeal of medieval monks.)

The book is a fast read, like a screenplay without those annoying camera directions. (And in fact, it started out as a screenplay, back in 1984.) The style will pull in readers who have never heard of McCarthy. Pared down, it eschews the baroque, elaborate, lengthy sentences characteristic of the author's previous fiction. But it is no less compelling. As usual, McCarthy refuses to use quotation marks, a practice that drives some readers away. I for one love it. James Joyce started this, or maybe Gertrude Stein, but at any rate it's a trademark of modernism, of which McCarthy is a sterling exemplar. (Actually, McCarthy has said he got the idea from MacKinlay Kantor's Civil War tale, *Andersonville,* a Pulitzer Prize–winning novel of 1955. Kantor's narrative works just fine without quotation marks.)

For die-hard McCarthy watchers, *No Country for Old Men* is a bit of a surprise. The word going round the Internet was that it was going to be set in New Orleans, but instead it takes place in far West Texas and is the closest thing to a straight-up genre novel that Cormac has written. The book begins with the voice of Ed Tom Bell, an old county sheriff: "I sent one boy to the gas chamber in Huntsville." (The gas chamber, incidentally, is a factual error. That method of execution has never been used at Huntsville.) The sheriff, a decorated World War II veteran who is haunted by a morally ambiguous action on the battlefield, is a decent man trying to protect the people of his county.

The Terrell County of the novel is a real county, down at the bottom of the Big Bend Canyon and bordered on the west by the Rio Grande. In 1982, near the time the novel is set, Terrell County had a population of 1,500. The county seat, Sanderson, where the sheriff's office is located, had a total population of 1,128 in 1990. In the 2010–2011 edition of *The Texas Almanac,* that number has slipped to 924. There's only one other town in the county, Dryden, which, to put it mildly, is not large. Dryden's population between the mid-1970s and the mid-1980s was forty-five; then, from 1988 to 2000, it has held at a rock steady 13. I am happy to report that at the end of 2009 it is still 13. The ethnic breakdown of the county as of 2007 was 47.7 percent Anglo, 0.00 percent Black, and 50.1 percent Hispanic. "Other" weighed in at 2.2 percent. The birth/death rate is stable. In 2006, 11 people were born in that county, and 11 died. There were five marriages and no divorces.

Since it's West Texas, the stereotypical view would be that it's cattle country, but that's not quite the case. In 1984, for example, the sheep and goat population of 162,000 far outnumbered cattle, pegged at 9,500. At the end of 2009 that figure has not changed appreciably. None of these animals figures in the narrative, but the facts are interesting anyway. In a sense the novel is an abattoir without cattle—humans are slaughtered with a pneumatic device used to kill beeves in slaughterhouses.

The sheriff's job is getting harder and harder, and the reader quickly understands why. Just two pages into the novel, we are introduced to one of Satan's chief subalterns, Anton Chigurh, he of the pneumatic device, an otherworldly psychopath possessed of a philosophical bent. His most immediate antecedent is Judge Holden, the inscrutable frontier polymath and scalp hunter in McCarthy's *Blood Meridian,* who stands for chaos incarnate. Flannery O'Connor's Misfit (from "A Good Man Is Hard to Find") is also relevant. The Misfit, another psychopath, is something of a hick theologian who's hung up on Jesus. Chigurh's philosophy doesn't come from Christianity but from a source that's not identified and is therefore sure to intrigue the intrepid McCarthy exegetes on the Internet. Chigurh's name, incidentally, is meant to sound like *sugar,* not *chigger,* which some reviewers thought it sounded like.

There is a fair amount of killing in the book, beginning on page six, when Chigurh kills a deputy sheriff in an interesting way. I count 27 violent human deaths, plus a dog's. This number may not be exact; sometimes a death is reported indirectly, a casual casualty. Of course, this is nothing compared with *Blood Meridian,* which in some sections averages about 27 deaths per paragraph, not counting mules. Those poor animals get shot; they fall off mountain paths; they die unnumbered though beautifully memorialized by McCarthy's prose.

To reveal whom Chigurh kills and why would be to violate the protocol of reviewing genre novels. The reader on the airplane does not want to know what happens in the book he is just opening, having purchased it just before boarding the plane; he wants to enjoy the thrill of the hunt. But I think it's permissible to recount the one instance when Chigurh decides *not* to kill somebody. (Still, it could have gone the other way.) He flips a coin to determine the fate of a filling station proprietor. The quarter bears the date 1958, and so he tells the man whose life hangs on the outcome of heads or tails: "It's been traveling twenty-two years to get here. And now it's here. And I'm here." Thus McCarthy precisely locates the action in time: 1980.

The third major character is Llewelyn Moss, a welder, good old boy, and former Vietnam sniper. (References to Vietnam abound.) Moss first appears very early in the novel. He is hunting antelope when he happens upon a "colossal goatf—k": a miniature massacre and $2.4 million in unmarked currency, a drug deal gone bad. (At this point, I'm fairly certain, the first Hollywood agent called about the rights. The reader starts casting it by page twenty. If they pick Wilfred Brimley to play the old sheriff, I'm never going to the movies again. (They didn't; they picked Tommy Lee Jones, who is perfect and didn't need to be coached on his accent.) Moss takes the money, an act that precipitates a prolonged and exciting chase.

McCarthy is a master of outdoors writing, and nobody captures Western spaces better. Here's a typical moment in which landscape and character are charged with meaning: "The sun was up less than an hour and the shadow of the ridge and the datilla and the rocks fell far out across the floodplain below him. Somewhere out there was the shadow of Moss himself." You could learn enough to pass a geology class just by looking up all the words for rocks and stony escarpments when McCarthy gets going: "talus," "scree," "lava scree," "barrial," "bajada," "caldera."

One of the keys to understanding the novel is its title, which is taken from the first line of William Butler Yeats's great poem "Sailing to Byzantium." I know this because as an undergraduate I memorized the poem and wrote a paper on it. The poem proposes that the solace of art transcends the natural world of procreation, fecundity, and death: "The young in one another's arms, birds in the trees / Those dying generations . . ." The first stanza stresses the constant life-death pulse of man's biological destiny, while the second offers the promise of something that outlasts the mutability of nature: the realm of art, symbolized by the splendors of the ancient city of Byzantium.

There are echoes of the Yeats poem in the novel. McCarthy's country is both that of the old sheriff and a desert landscape with a history of violence stretching back into the unrecorded past. Instead of a city of great beauty (after all, we are talking about West Texas here), McCarthy's example of man's ability to make something imperishable in that harsh land is a stone water trough that Sheriff Bell remembers from his past. He marvels at the patience and labor it took to carve the trough, the years of faithful dedication to make something that would last "ten thousand years." The house that once stood near where it lies, the people, the stone carver, are all long gone. The only thing

that remains is the trough, and to Bell it signifies that for its arti-
san, "there was some sort of promise in his heart."

Intermittently, in thirteen numbered monologues, we are immersed in the mind of Bell, who believes that the world, specifically America, is undergoing some kind of change for the worse.
The part of the world he knows best is being overrun by strange
new forces hostile to everything sane and normal. Drugs and
drug dealing and the violence they engender are the central and
presumably insoluble problems underlying the book's action.

Bell's meditations, as it were, are theological. Pondering
whether Satan exists, he decides that very possibly he does, and
he is certain that the worship of mammon is the nation's true
religion.

The politics of the novel are right of center. Bell is anti-
abortion, anti-drugs, and anti-kids who dye their hair green and
put bones in their noses. He thinks the disintegration of civic
polity is much advanced. He thinks things begin to fall apart
when people stop using ordinary manners. Here is Bell answer-
ing a reporter's question: "Sheriff, how come you to let crime
get so out of hand in your county? Sounded like a fair question
I reckon. Maybe it was a fair question. Anyway I told her, I said:
It starts when you begin to overlook bad manners. Any time you
quit hearin Sir and Mam the end is pretty much in sight. I told
her, I said: It reaches into ever strata. You've heard about that
ain't you? Ever strata? You finally get into the sort of breakdown
in mercantile ethics that leaves people settin around out in the
desert dead in their vehicles and by then it's just too late." A re-
viewer for the *New Yorker* said he didn't think a sheriff in West
Texas would use the words "mercantile ethics," but what does he
know?

I don't want to make Bell sound like some grim, pitchfork-
wielding, *American Gothic* right-winger type. He's not; he has
a perfect-pitch sense of humor and is awfully hard on himself
for past failings, but he is seriously worried about the direction
things are headed.

More than any of McCarthy's previous novels, this one is
saturated with the news of the day, in this case, the late Carter

era. There is a reference to the murder of a federal judge. That would be Judge John Wood, who was gunned down in San Antonio by movie star Woody Harrelson's father. (That Woody Harrelson was cast in the film adds a nice after-the-fact irony.) Bell reads a newspaper account that confirms his pessimism about the nation's drift toward violence. The story, which seems to derive from one that was widely circulated in the national press, compares a questionnaire from the thirties concerning the conduct of children in the public schools with a similar one in recent times. The problems had shifted from chewing gum and running in the hall to murder and rape. Now, what's interesting about this, from a political point of view, is the lengths to which liberals like Molly Ivins and Lou Dubose went, in the first of their seventy-four books about George W. Bush, to establish that this old story is an urban myth. Can an urban myth be true? Other myths are true, the claim is made by such towering intellects as Bill Moyers, if they're classical or tribal or Jungian and endorsed by Joseph Campbell. So why not an urban myth? Is there not some underlying truth to Bell's (and therefore McCarthy's) use of this story? In the 1950s when I was in high school, the truth of that "myth" was apparent. There were no drugs, no homicidal attacks on teachers and students. Public schools, at least in my experience, were not likely to become crime scenes. Maybe it was different other places. One of my favorite films of my teenage years, *Blackboard Jungle,* certainly painted a worrisome world of urban gangs and rape and violence, but that was in New York City. That kind of stuff hadn't reached the public schools of the provinces yet.

McCarthy's body of published work now consists of ten novels and a couple of plays. Among his pre-Southwestern works, the two most highly regarded are *Child of God* (1973) and *Suttree* (1979). Among the Westerns the undoubted masterpiece is *Blood Meridian* (1985). No less an arbiter of canonicity than Yale literary Brahmin Harold Bloom favors *Blood Meridian,* and I have no reason to argue with him. Bloom rates it the only post–World War II work comparable to the best of Herman Melville and William Faulkner and ahead of anything by Thomas Pynchon,

Don DeLillo, or Philip Roth. *All the Pretty Horses* (1992) and *The Crossing* (1994), the first two of the Border Trilogy, have many, many fans.

No Country for Old Men will not alter these rankings, but it is well worth reading for those with a taste for style, violence, and philosophical ponderings. To me, Bell is crucial to the novel. Without Bell, the novel is simply a noir thriller. But Bell's forebodings, his absolute certitude that evil, however mysterious, certainly does exist, his very seriousness—all of this deepens and extends the novel beyond the predictable boundaries of the thriller. And it becomes clearer every day that the prophetic aspects of the novel are amply borne out in the recent eruptions of drug-related violence in the "running borderlands" of northern Mexico and Texas.

2005

This novel of course went on to become a succès d'estime when filmed by the Coen Bros and took home the Oscar for Best Picture in 2006.

In 2009 the Southwestern Writers Collection at the Alkek Library of Texas State University acquired Cormac McCarthy's archives for 2.something million dollars, and so it is now possible to follow the paper trail of his works from early drafts to the published text. I spent part of a day in late 2009 examining materials relating to *No Country for Old Men*. Here are some items from that perusal:

1. McCarthy tried out a number of versions of his killer's name until he arrived at a keeper: Chingerst, Chinorste, Chignon, Chigover, Chigney, Chisgore. For a while, in one of the typescripts, the name is Chignon. Then finally it is Chigurh.
2. There is a strange scene that takes place in Black River Falls, Wisconsin, on December 18, 1973. An unidentified male, a hunter, meditates upon the figure of a beautiful woman hanging in a tree amidst the snow.
3. There is a passage about the legal rights that Adolph Hitler would be entitled to if he were being held in an American prison.
4. In a section titled "Prison," Bell learns that Chigurh, awaiting execu-

tion, dies of "causes unknown." The official report, because there has to be one, will state heart attack as the cause of death. At one point Bell says to the doctor, "I know he's dead, Doc. I think my problem is I don't know what it is that died." Bell asks about the autopsy and the doctor reports that there was nothing "abnormal" about his brain. Bell opens one eye, then the other of the dead Chigurh but can see nothing in them to explain the source of that evil.

To me this is the most interesting single section in the archives on this novel. Such an ending to the novel would have satisfied those viewers of the film who were disappointed that the good guy didn't vanquish the bad guy.

5. But surely the strangest section of the unpublished fragments relating to the novel is a one-page scene titled "Kid." In this scene a strange kid acting as a kind of psychiatrist questions a female subject: Did he attempt to slobber upon your clamlet? Was there digital exploration? To which she responds, None of the above.

DEAR CORMAC

A couple of years ago the Texas Book Festival "Bookended" you. (They will Bookend anybody, so it's nothing to feel cocky about.) Since you famously do not appear in person to receive awards and over the years have kept yourself as invisible as some desert prophet living among burning, barren latitudes of the Southwest, I was asked to say a few words on your behalf. So although I had to give up my regular Saturday morning Muny golf match and appear in your stead, I was okay with that; I was willing to do my bit for Literature.

In my remarks to the swells at the book festival, I depicted you and me as buddies who e-mailed each other all the time. Maybe they believed me. I said that you always began with "Hi Don" and tried to pass yourself off as some macho dude just back from a weekend of tequila-crawling in Juárez but that I knew differently. I knew that you really spent your weekends peddling *Blood Meridian* T-shirts on the plaza in front of the cathedral in Santa Fe. Turns out I wasn't that far off.

Among most authors it is part of the trade to give readings, and this is one thing you have never done. Having seen and heard many authors over the years, I can report that such readings are among the most disappointing forms of literary interaction. Incidentally, I feel like I'm in good company on this point. Larry McMurtry has recently observed, "I like to read what writers write but am rarely in the mood to listen to them yap." In thinking about all of the authors I have heard—and that number would be in the hundreds—there are only four who were truly memorable: William Burroughs, Jamaica Kincaid, Marie Howe, and George Plimpton. That's it; that's the lot. So it never bothered me that you, Cormac, never gave readings. In fact, it pleased me. I thought your nonparticipation in such events was in your favor. I admired you for not trucking around the country hawking your books.

Then came your appearance on *Oprah*. Out here in McCarthy-land we're still trying to take it in.

The only *Oprah* show I ever saw until the one you were on was in 1991, in Sydney, Australia. It was a really good show. It was before she became spiritual and all New Age-y. What it was was a show about incest. She brought these fat white trash girls from the South (the home of incest) on stage and let them tell their stories of how their daddies had molested them and everything. It was pretty disgusting. But what was great was, then she brought out all the daddies and they shuffled on stage wearing their gimme caps and looking sheepish and a little proud, too, at being on *Oprah* and all, and the girls all cried and hugged their daddies, who continued to look sheepish and proud. It was better than *Deliverance*.

So that's all I have to compare the show you were on with, and I gotta tell you, yours was really boring. And kind of embarrassing, I thought, because the first thing Oprah did was to tell us how she gave you a 24-hour ultimatum and how you caved in when she called back. A lifetime of committed artistic celibacy, and in one phone call you're in an oversized chair out there at the Institute and Oprah is talking to you on TV for all the world to see. It won't be in the Golden Age of TV Archives, I can assure you. But it is on YouTube and anybody can download it if they're of a mind. Personally, I prefer the Penélope Cruz make-out session with her sister, but for those of a middlebrow literary bent, YouTube will do.

Let me review your performance. You were cute, cuddly, and comfortable. You even giggled. And when Oprah was done with you, I half expected to see America's greatest outdoor novelist crawl into her lap and take a nap on her ample breasts. (The only thing to match this, I imagine, would be a double-shot Buttery Nipple.)

What did we learn from seeing you on *Oprah?* That you believe that all we really need are food and shoes. That you consider yours to have been a lucky life. That you prefer left-brain types to the artsy crowd. That you don't care who reads your books. This shocked Oprah, but here was a glimmer of the tough guy I was hoping for. We learned almost nothing about the novel. When Oprah asked you a simple question — What is the significance of the time 1:17 in the novel (when the lights go out for good)? — you said you didn't know. You missed an opportunity here. You could have sent us scurrying to that bit in Revelations or the Gospels that would have unlocked everything.

I know the *Oprah* thing was about money, and on one level I certainly don't hold you, to use one of your favorite words, "accountable." I personally would crawl to Chicago to be on *Oprah* to sell books. I could hear cash registers spitting out receipts all over America as Oprah's followers rushed out to get their kicks on Cormac's Route 666.

Incidentally, what I would like to see is a follow-up study of how many of Oprah's followers *actually read* the novel.

Where once your legion of fans could count on your fidelity to artistic anonymity, now we see your phiz everywhere. For a long while, when I thought of reclusive American writers, three names came instantly to mind: J. D. Salinger, Thomas Pynchon, and Cormac McCarthy. The first managed to stay out of the public eye until a former lover wrote a tell-all memoir, permanently damaging his cult of secrecy. And although the second remains as little known as the Unabomber before he was captured, his work has deteriorated so steadily that no one even cares where he's hiding anymore.

That left us with you, or it did until you appeared on *Oprah.* Pre-*Oprah,* the thing I loved about you was that you were a true mystery man. You didn't give readings or do signings or appear in public; you didn't attend writers' conferences; you didn't even take visiting writer positions at universities, the easiest money there is. You were a ghost who wrote like a dream, a Bartleby who preferred not to show himself, and I loved you for it. Authors are the opposite of children: they should be read and not seen.

Remember how it used to be? In the beginning, you were mostly rumor, some unknown plowman working the burned-over ground not finished off by Faulkner and Flannery O'Connor, some faceless hewer of prose and spiller of blood. In 1976 you moved to Texas, to El Paso, and nine years later, without much fanfare, out popped *Blood Meridian,* the novel that most critics consider your greatest. Harvard doyen Harold Bloom thinks it belongs right there in the pantheon with *Moby-Dick* and *As I Lay Dying.* But you didn't take a victory lap or give us a curtain call. It hit the same year as Larry McMurtry's *Lonesome Dove,* probably the all-time favorite novel of Texas readers, and James Michener's solemn, unreadable tome *Texas,* which was supposed to be—the governor said so—the big book to celebrate the state's sesquicentennial. Each of those books sold millions of copies, but *Blood Meridian* sold only about 1,200 in hardback. But sales are not everything. The book acquired a cult following and set scholars and amateurs alike chasing down its arcane language and historical sources in a hunt for its ultimate meaning. It was a book for the ages.

You stuck to your guns, even as your Border Trilogy started piling up sales in the nineties and your reputation and readership grew. In the late 1990s I won second place in a Bad Cormac Contest (modeled on the famous Bad Hemingway parody contests) and flew to El Paso to collect my modest prize, a copy of one of your plays that I have not yet read. I did not expect you to appear, and you did not, thus fulfilling my deepest fantasy.

Through the years of mounting fame and financial success you maintained your policy of disengagement; you declined to give readings or appear at conferences; you remained out of view, and dammit, I admired that. I admired it so much that in 2000, at a meeting of a Texas Writers Month committee to select a writer to be honored—a very amateurish promotional idea in the main—I nominated you. Someone asked if you were a "nurturer." I nearly choked. I told them you had better things to do; you were a writer, not a uniter.

In my class at the University of Texas on southwestern lit I purveyed such sparse anecdotes as were shared by Cormackians on CormacMcCarthy.com or by other interested parties. I explained how there were two sides to your mysterious persona—the tough hombre, who could describe massacres so coldly and eloquently that I wanted to see more dead babies hung by their lips on cactus thorns, and the purist, the last high priest of modernism, heir to Joyce's robes. The only person of my acquaintance who has met you is Tom Staley, the director of the Harry Ransom Center, at the University of Texas. According to Staley, all you would talk about over dinner was *Dubliners*. You quoted sentences from Joyce's great collection of stories and queried Tom, a Joyce scholar, on what this word meant, what that word meant.

Those were the good years. You just wrote. That was all you needed to do; it is what you were born for.

After *Oprah*, each public sighting downsized your legend. There you were in *Time*, being interviewed alongside the cute little Coen brothers. How depressing. You said you really liked their film *Miller's Crossing*. Great. I don't want to know that. Couldn't you have mentioned *Blood Simple*? At least that would have evoked your greatest novel, reminding us that you were, after all, still the Man.

And then there was the *Rolling Stone* article about life at the Santa Fe Institute, the interdisciplinary New Mexico think tank where you've been in residence off and on since 1988. Let me tell you something: The rest of us losers are tired of hearing about this place. I don't care what cutting-edge scientists think. I'm trying to make a living. Leave me alone about quarks and plagues. I'll deal with them when they show up. The worst part of that article was learning that you bus the food trays after those scintillating lunches. Are you kidding me? Let the freaking scientists bus their own trays. Let them get a government grant.

Also, it was sobering to learn that you haven't had a drink in thirty years. That's a long time.

By the time the Oscars rolled around for *No Country for Old Men,* seeing you in celeb circles was old hat. And sure enough, there you were on Oscar night, seated amongst the stars. It was just a cutaway shot, but it was enough.

Cormac, I'm really looking forward to your next novel, as always. As you told us in a recent interview in the *Wall Street Journal* (2009), it's set in New Orleans. Rumors of this novel have been out there for a while. We're ready.

But please, whatever happens, don't do *The View.* I'm begging you.

Your pal,
Don

2008

Reaction to this *Texas Monthly* column was radically divided. Some readers really liked it, but those who did not went berserk in their letters to the editor. Such readers were, I believe, either unfamiliar with or uncomfortable with irony and satire. The two most outraged (and outrageous) letters were postmarked El Paso, where McCarthy lived for a number of years. One was from a guy who had never heard of Cormac McCarthy and couldn't figure out why *Texas Monthly* would publish something about a nobody by a nobody. The other was from an old bird who has been a member of the Texas Institute of Letters for about a hundred years. It was a three-page handwritten missive, and you could smell the cordite on the page. What I had written was, gasp, *unconscionable.* He demanded that I issue a public apology to Cormac. Instead I have reprinted here a revised version of the *TM* piece that is closer to my original draft and which makes perfectly clear, except perhaps to those who are hopelessly obtuse, my admiration for McCarthy's fiction.

Since Cormac's emergence into the glare of publicity, he has continued to appear now and then in print venues. He gave an interview to the *Wall Street Journal* in November 2009, for example, in connection with the release of the film *The Road,* based on his Pulitzer Prize–winning novel of 2007. One thing he said is puzzling. When asked about why he had moved to the Southwest, McCarthy responded, "I ended up in the Southwest because I knew that nobody had ever written about it." He added, "But nobody had taken it seriously, not in 200 years. I thought, here's a good subject. And it was." Such a statement might come as a bit of a surprise to Willa Cather, William Eastlake, Max Evans, and scores of other Southwestern writers, including, most of all, Larry McMurtry. It's hard to know if this is ignorance on McCarthy's part (which I seriously doubt), thoughtlessness, or egotism.

In contrast, McMurtry has been quite generous in comments he has made about McCarthy's work. In "A River Runs Through It" (*Newsweek,* Nov. 5, 2007), McMurtry calls McCarthy "the literary master of the border." Continuing, McMurtry describes the world of *No Country for Old Men* with the authority of one who knows that culture well: "It's not only no country for old men; it's no country for young or middle-aged men, either. It's also hard on dogs, and hardest on women." McMurtry's praise of Cormac is a particularly generous act because McCarthy is the best writer to inhabit the literary landscape of West Texas since . . . Larry McMurtry.

One final note. The latest McCarthy item to make news is his typewriter, an Olivetti Lettera 32 that he bought for $50 in Knoxville, Tennessee, in 1963. It is estimated that he has written 5 million words on this machine. Sold at auction in December 2009, the now-legendary Olivetti fetched $254,500, which was donated to the Santa Fe Institute. Cormac's new typewriter is another Olivetti.

PART III *Discontents*

WAYNE'S WORLD

When John Wayne died, in 1979, an Austin TV news anchor called me to get my thoughts on Wayne as a Texan. I said he wasn't any more a Texan than Davy Crockett was, but later I reconsidered. Davy Crockett became a Texan by dying at the Alamo, and John Wayne became a Texan by making *The Alamo,* the biggest film ever about the fateful battle. "Big" was the word from the start. The year they shot the film, 1959, Texas needed to be reminded of its outsized history because, on January 3, Alaska had entered the Union.

It was Texas chauvinism that got the film made here in the first place. The shocking truth is that Wayne, who had been interested in filming the Alamo story as far back as 1945, had searched for locations in South America and Mexico. At one point he was close to settling on Panama, which had San Antonio–like scenery and even cheaper labor. Later he seriously considered Durango, Mexico, a site that John Huston would use for *The Unforgiven* the same year Wayne made *The Alamo.* Alarmed at the thought of the state's mythic battle being reenacted in Mexico, prominent Texans—including Bob O'Donnell, who owned a chain of movie theaters—said no way, José, and let it be known that they wouldn't permit the film to be distributed in the state if it was shot in Mexico.

Wayne got the message. Fortunately, a site was waiting for him: James T. "Happy" Shahan's 22,000-acre ranch, located north of Brackettville in the spare brush country 130 miles west of San Antonio and 40 miles from the border. Shahan, an eager-beaver rancher-turned-promoter, had already lured one film company to Brackettville. In 1955 Wayne's old studio, Republic, had come to town to shoot *The Last Command,* starring Sterling Hayden as a wooden Jim Bowie and Arthur Hunnicutt as a grizzled-old-coot Davy Crockett. TV's bland Richard (*I Led Three Lives*) Carlson played Colonel Travis.

The Last Command was the film Wayne had wanted to make when he was under contract to Republic—even hiring his pal James Edward Grant to write a script in 1950—but studio head Herbert Yates kept putting him off. John Ford, the great director who in 1939 had lifted Wayne out of the doldrums of B shoot-'em-ups to star in *Stagecoach* and then had made him the centerpiece of his cavalry trilogy (*Fort Apache, She Wore a Yellow Ribbon,* and *Rio Grande*), had been in line to direct Wayne in the Alamo film at Republic. But Yates stalled, and in 1951 Wayne left and formed his own production company. Yates held on to the Grant script, however, and the film he signed off on, *The Last Command,* appears to be a rewrite of it. According to several Wayne biographers, Yates made *The Last Command* as much to get back at him for deserting Republic as anything else.

In 1957 Happy Shahan invited Wayne to Texas to scout the Brackettville location. Wayne brought along his art designer, Al Ybarra, and they both liked what they saw. Wayne wanted a lot of empty space around the Alamo, and the real site, in the heart of downtown San Antonio, wouldn't work at all. Here, however, were miles and miles of empty Texas hardscrabble just waiting for a Hollywood makeover.

The decision to shoot at Brackettville meant that Wayne's long-standing desire to direct a film about the Alamo was · finally going to be realized. No one is sure when the actor first fell under the sway of the Alamo story, the foundation narrative so central to Texas history. He may have heard about it from John Ford's brother Francis, who had appeared in the first Alamo movie, *The Immortal Alamo,* filmed in San Antonio in 1911, or perhaps from Bob Steele, a friend who had been in the 1926 silent *Davy Crockett at the Fall of the Alamo.* In any event, for Wayne the story of the 180 or more Texians who, in late February and early March of 1836, had held out for thirteen days against overwhelming odds and sacrificed their lives for Texas, contained themes that went far beyond those of local interest. To Wayne the story of the Alamo was nothing less than the story of America, of the nation's absolute commitment to freedom. According to a 1958 article in the *San Antonio Light,* he considered it "the greatest piece of folklore ever brought down through history. The Alamo is real Americana. Those fellas were real heroes."

Once again, Wayne turned to his old friend James Edward Grant to write a script that would breathe life into those heroes. Finally, after more than a decade of worrying about *The Alamo*— the first film he would direct—the project was under way. It was truly a Texas-size undertaking. In late 1957 construction began on the false-front Alamo and the town of San Antonio de Béxar, which eventually boasted nineteen buildings. Workers from Mexico were brought in to make adobe bricks, and things went well until a twenty-inch rainfall destroyed 32,000 bricks and almost washed away the little make-believe town. Engineers went to work and built a drainage system to prevent future muddy disasters.

The quest for authenticity became a theme of the movie's press releases, which would exhibit a pattern of PR deception and exaggeration that would culminate in the over-the-top rhetoric of the Oscars campaign. A typical example: It was reported that Ybarra wanted the Alamo to be so historically accurate that he traveled to Spain to research the original architectural plans. Ybarra didn't go to Spain, of course, but he did do a good job of constructing the Alamo's facade, although one of Wayne's last-minute touches violated the historical record in favor of "art." Wayne ordered Ybarra to take down a small cross on top of the chapel and "gimme something allegorical," a larger cross. Ybarra did, and went Wayne one better by tilting it on its side, a fallen cross. The effect was striking. The film is full of crosses, a bit of iconography Wayne probably learned from the Catholic Ford. Historical authenticity apparently wasn't as crucial when it came to building the fake town of San Antonio. Bearing no resemblance at all to the real San Antonio, it looked instead like the conventional Western town of a thousand movies, probably because Happy Shahan wanted a generic town for all the films that might be shot on his ranch in the future.

In all, it took two years to get everything built, and ongoing problems with financing added to the delays. But Wayne kept busy during 1958, shooting *The Barbarian and the Geisha, Rio Bravo,* and *The Horse Soldiers*—and he was constantly on the phone, working on *The Alamo* long distance.

Finally, on September 9, 1959, shooting officially commenced. Things got off to a good start, but then, at the end of the first week, Happy Shahan's daughter was seriously injured in a head-on collision with some crew members from Wayne's production company, Batjac, who were returning from Del Rio. She eventually recovered, but a few weeks later real tragedy struck. A young actress named Lagene Ethridge, a member of a traveling stock company called the Hollywood Starlight Players, gave a reading for a small part and so impressed Wayne that he signed her up to play a frontier woman. This looked like Ethridge's big break. She and the rest of her company, including her boyfriend, Chester Harvey Smith, were staying in Spofford, a little south of Brackettville. When Ethridge's role required her to move to Fort Clark in Brackettville for two weeks, Smith wasn't happy. They had a fight about it, and as she was preparing to leave, he plunged a twelve-inch butcher knife into her abdomen, killing her.

Saddened over the death of the promising young actress and harassed by reporters trying to exploit the story, Wayne was alarmed to learn that Smith's lawyer had subpoenaed him to testify at a hearing. Wayne had state troopers set up roadblocks in South Texas to find the lawyer, and when they did, inquired why on earth he was being asked to testify. Because he was Ethridge's employer, the lawyer said. The film was costing approximately $60,000 a day, and to avoid further delays, Wayne gave a deposition in Brackettville. He was angry about the death and angry about being tied up in the proceedings. He told the press he thought Smith should be executed, but the killer got twenty years instead.

After the flood, the near-fatal accident, and the murder, the Fort Clark offices of Batjac and the movie's publicity staff caught on fire, destroying a lot of promotional materials and records. Other problems popped up. Texas critters abounded in the wild country where they were filming, and rattlesnakes proved the most populous and persistent. A cannon rolled over Laurence Harvey's foot. Eighty percent of the cast and crew came down with the flu.

Then there were the visitors who had to be looked after and who took up valuable time. John Ford's arrival created nothing but problems for Wayne. It is certain that Wayne didn't want Ford on the set looking over his shoulder. This was Wayne's film, not Ford's. Wayne couldn't bring himself to order the great man off the set, so he came up with a plan: He gave Ford some second-unit action sequences to film and sent him off to do it out of sight. Ford filmed several scenes but later stated pointedly that none of them appeared in the film. Wayne didn't want anybody later saying that Ford was the real director of *The Alamo*.

Another famous visitor was J. Frank Dobie, the state's resident authority on everything Texan. Accompanied by his future biographer, Lon Tinkle, himself the author of a stirring Alamo book (*Thirteen Days to Glory*), Dobie happened to be present when Wayne was filming the arrival of a herd of three hundred Texas longhorns. Bill Daniel, the brother of Governor Price Daniel, had gone to considerable effort to find so many of the storied breed, and Dobie was greatly moved at the sight. Wayne, who saw a tear on the old man's face, asked him what was the matter, and Dobie replied, "We'll never see the great longhorns again in number like this."

There were other visitors. Laurence Harvey's wife, British actress Margaret Leighton, spent a few days in Brackettville. When Harvey had told her that he was going to make the film, she had asked, "Darling, what's an Alamo?"

The officers of the Daughters of the Republic of Texas, the

official custodians of the real Alamo, visited Duke on the set and had their photograph taken with him. Another day, eight winners of a "Remember the Alamo" radio contest dropped by. Governor Daniel also visited the set. The greatest Longhorn of them all, Coach Darrell Royal, along with twelve fellow gridiron gurus, landed on the set's airstrip in a private plane and spent part of a day looking around. Then, in late December, after eighty-three days of shooting, the film was completed.

Wayne had made one of the most expensive movies in motion picture history up to that point, costing an estimated $10 million to $12 million. Now came the selling of *The Alamo*, and for a big job like that Wayne called on Russell Birdwell, a native Texan PR maven whose slogan was "I can make anyone famous—for the right fee." Birdwell, who had made his reputation plugging *Gone with the Wind* and *The Outlaw*, Howard Hughes's soporific dog-and-pony show Western, plunged into the campaign at warp speed and never let up. One of the first things he did was to write United Artists, the film's distributor, claiming that the Battle of the Alamo was "the greatest single event, perhaps, that has transpired since they nailed Christ to the cross."

One of Birdwell's projects was a press kit that was so big—184 pages—it was promptly dubbed "the bible." The bible specialized in stats, reporting trivia as though they bore some revelatory meaning. During the eighty-three days of filming, for example, the cast and crew consumed 192,509 "savory meals" and gulped down 510,000 cups of coffee, 900 gallons of ice cream, 53,000 steaks, and 12,500 pounds of "miscellaneous meat" (roadkill?). The list went on. Birdwell was a chronicler of so-what facts and measurements: the production set required 10 miles of underground wiring, 14 miles of new roads, 6 deep wells that pumped forth 25,000 gallons of pure artesian water each day, 40 miles of reinforced construction steel, 12 miles of water pipes, 30,000 square feet of imported Spanish tile, and—probably the most important detail of all, considering the place and time, Texas in September—$75,000 worth of portable air-conditioning equipment. If it could be quantified, Birdwell counted it. If it could be exaggerated, Birdwell did.

Before the film's world premiere, held in San Antonio on October 24, 1960, Birdwell made waves in the political world, prompted perhaps by Wayne's insistence on the film's transcendent relevance to world affairs. Wayne conceived of *The Alamo* as a cold war anthem of American resolve. "I don't think it belongs to Texans alone," he declared in Birdwell's monumental press kit. "It belongs to people everywhere who value the priceless treasure of freedom." In his book *John Wayne's America,* Garry Wills goes so far as to say that "the closest Wayne came to having a real religion, one for which he would sacrifice himself, was his devotion to the Alamo."

Birdwell's ambitions for the film knew no bounds. He tried to get Congress to award the Congressional Medal of Honor to all of the defenders of the Alamo. Even more grandiosely, he wrote the president of the Daughters of the Republic of Texas, urging that the leaders of France, the Soviet Union, England, and the United States hold their next summit meeting in the Alamo. Governor Daniel put the kibosh on that plan, writing Birdwell that he should drop the summit idea because "you won't find many people who would like for Khrushchev to visit our State—much less attend a meeting in the Alamo." In the same letter, the governor also wanted to make sure that his brother, Bill, received screen credit for a few on-camera lines delivered early in the film.

Undeterred, the irrepressible Birdwell had another nifty idea, this time for the souvenir program to be handed out at the world premiere, and to that end he wrote Sir Winston Churchill requesting that he write a hundred-word foreword, with an appropriate fee to be awarded to a charity of Churchill's choosing. The former prime minister of Great Britain and Nobel Prize winner declined.

After the premiere of *The Alamo,* Birdwell trained his guns on securing Academy Awards for the movie, a campaign in which the publicist outdid himself in overreaching and wretched excess. The film had garnered seven Oscar nominations, including Best Picture (though not Best Director). With Wayne in Africa shooting *Hatari,* Birdwell flew wild and free. In a controversial move he sent letters to Academy members implying that it would be unpatriotic to vote for any other film. Journalists mocked Birdwell's heavy-handed tactics, and Wayne returned in time to help suppress the firestorm of criticism.

Then along came Chill Wills, who had received a Best Supporting Actor nomination for his portrayal of Beekeeper, a fictional character who pals around with Wayne's Crockett in the film. Wills got a bad case of Oscar fever. In a clumsy attempt to influence the voting, his publicist, W. S. "Bow Wow" Wojciechowicz, placed ads in the Hollywood trades listing hundreds of Academy members and referring to them, in Wills's cornball fashion, as the actor's "cousins." Groucho Marx took out a retaliatory ad in *Variety:* "Dear Mr. Chill Wills, I Am Delighted to Be Your Cousin, but I Voted for Sal Mineo." (Mineo was nominated for his role in *Exodus.)* The ad that drove John Wayne into a fury appeared in the *Hollywood Reporter:* "We of the *Alamo* cast are praying harder than the real Texans prayed for their lives in the Alamo for Chill Wills to win the Oscar." Wayne himself placed an ad in the *Reporter* denouncing the tactics of the Wills camp.

After all that, *The Alamo* took home one Oscar—for Best Sound. But it was by no means the commercial or critical disaster it has sometimes been called. It was the number-seven top grosser the year of its release, earning $8 million, and it did especially well in Japan, England, and other foreign markets. It won several film awards from such organizations as *Good Housekeeping Magazine,* the Hollywood Foreign Press Association, and the National Cowboy Hall of Fame and Western Heritage Center in Oklahoma City.

While native sons and daughters were able to work up a lot of patriotic enthusiasm for the film, the more discerning among them were also amused by its ridiculous errors. James Edward Grant, who always stressed his commitment to historical accuracy, bragged that he'd read everything about the Alamo. Maybe so, but why then did he place the old mission on the banks of the Rio Grande instead of where it belongs, on the San Antonio River, a mischarting of some two hundred miles? Nearly all of the film's geography is screwy. At one point help is said to be coming from Goliad in the north, but Goliad, of course, is southeast of San Antonio. There are many other inaccuracies as well. Davy Crockett, for example, is given a completely made-up love interest—Flaca, played by Linda Cristal—and the death of James Bowie's wife is reported in the movie when in fact she died three years before the battle.

But in the end, none of that mattered. *The Alamo* wasn't history; it was a sentimental ballad or, better yet, a sermon about freedom, the Cold War, the concept of a republic, and a bunch of other Big Ideas that are in there somewhere. As Duke put it years later, "There's more to that movie than my damn conservative attitude."

2000

The title was the first thing I thought of when I was assigned this piece, and it survived the editorial process.

Chill Wills's son, William Wills of Dallas, wrote an interesting letter to *Texas Monthly,* pointing out that his father probably got the idea of promoting his candidacy for an Academy Award from the example of Michael Todd, who, back in 1956, "bought the Oscar" for *Around the World in Eighty Days.* Its chief competitor that year? *Giant,* in which Chill Wills thought that he should have won an Oscar for Best Supporting Actor.

PICTURE PERFECT

In the fall of 1970 the magic of Hollywood descended on Archer City, Texas, population 1,722. Director Peter Bogdanovich, 31, arrived with the cast and crew to begin shooting Larry McMurtry's *The Last Picture Show,* a bittersweet, no-holds-barred story about growing up in Texas in the fifties. Tongue firmly in cheek, McMurtry had "lovingly dedicated" the novel to his hometown, and many of its citizens had not forgotten. Ministers railed and townspeople arched their brows at the sinfulness of this "dirty" book, which McMurtry's mother later admitted she had hidden in the closet. And now, adding insult to injury, they were making a moving picture to go with it. One letter to the local newspaper spoke of both the end of an era and the wayward day dawning on the horizon, where wicked larger towns like Wichita Falls loomed: "I, for one, feel that Archer City will come out of this with a sickness in it's [*sic*] stomach and a certain misgiving about the support the City is lending to the further degradation and decay of the morals and attitudes we foist upon our youth in this County."

Undeterred, Bogdanovich and company persevered, and after ten weeks of production and a year of cutting by the director, their joint effort yielded an American masterpiece. (In 1991 Bogdanovich restored seven minutes of footage cut from the original film—three scenes in all—for a laser disc letterbox edition.) *The Last Picture Show* won eight Academy Award nominations and garnered Oscars for Ben Johnson and Cloris Leachman (best supporting actor and actress). The film also won three British Academy Awards, one Golden Globe Award, seven New York Film Critics Awards, and one National Society of Film Critics Award. In 1998 the Library of Congress selected it for the National Film Registry.

A film is the result of a vast collaboration over time, and what happens off camera can have a crucial impact on what happens on-screen. On the set of *The Last Picture Show,* the private lives of the actors intersected with those of the characters they depicted; passions swirled around the picture with the same force as the winds that blew through the empty streets of the little Texas town. How the movie was made is a story best told by the participants: Peter Bogdanovich (director), Cybill Shepherd (Jacy Farrow), Timothy Bottoms (Sonny Crawford), Jeff Bridges (Duane Jackson), Cloris Leachman (Ruth Popper), Eileen Brennan (Genevieve), Sam Bottoms (Billy), Polly Platt (production designer), and Gary Chason (assistant to the director). In 1999 I conducted interviews in person or by phone with the principal Hollywood folks who made *The Last Picture Show.* To me, their stories are as interesting as the film they made.

THE PLACE

Bogdanovich: Well, the truth is that Archer City sort of picked us. We went down to look at locations, and Larry had volunteered to take us around Texas—he loves to drive around—so he drove me and the production designer, Polly Platt [Bogdanovich's wife at the time], around. He met us at the Dallas airport, and he said, "Where you wanna go? You wanna go north or south? You wanna go to Archer City?" And I said, "Well, let's go there last. Let's see everything else that there is," thinking that probably Archer City wouldn't even be right. I thought, "That'd be his hometown. Why would that be right?" So we spent a couple of days driving around Texas, more than a couple of days, and we said, "Let's fly back to Dallas and drive up to Archer City." And the minute we drove into town, the minute I could see that stoplight blinking at me, and it was kinda getting a little late as we drove in, I said, "This is it." And Larry of course said, "Well, it oughta be. It's the town I wrote about."

Platt: I was asleep in the back seat listening to Larry and Peter in the front talking about the movie, and I would sort of go to sleep and wake up and listen to their murmuring voices. It was very, very special. And we got into the town—it was a stormy, rainy, sleety March—and the town was as gray and ugly as you've ever seen. There were tumbleweeds blowing through the town; it was closed down. And we saw that it had the tank dam, it had the lake, it had the high school, it had the square—and even though the main square needed a lot of work, we decided to do it. We decided to do it there.

Bridges: It's funny. When you're making a movie like that, the place you're shooting almost seems like a set. That whole town, we used that whole town as a big set, basically.

Brennan: Shooting in the town did a lot of the work for the actors because the town is extremely bleak.

Bogdanovich: They were not happy that we were there. They did not like the book; the town was hostile to the book, which by the way had not been a successful book. I don't believe it sold more than about six thousand copies in hardcover. So the success of the picture and Larry's subsequent success made Archer City like us a lot better when we went back for *Texasville.*

Platt: I remember we went into the McMurtry house, and Jeff McMurtry, Larry's father, instead of saying hello to Larry— Larry said, "This is Polly and Peter," and Hazel [his mother] was all friendly and everything, and she gave us a pecan pie—Jeff McMurtry just came right over to me and was looking at Larry, and instead of saying "How do you do?" or "Nice to meet you," or the usual Texas thing, he said, "You know what?"—he was looking at Larry—"You pour kerosene on him, and I'll light the match."

Leachman: This is a very hard-bitten place; you felt the lives, living there. It's so painful. I mean it's so, what do they call it? Quiet desperation. Everybody knows everybody. I don't know if you can really share when you have to protect your pride. I think that's why it can be awfully lonely if you feel you can't share, like my character. Ruth had nobody to share with, nor did she even think she had the right to feel she was suffering at all; that was her lot in life.

Chason: Since *The Last Picture Show* and McMurtry's work are so rooted in the land, so site specific, I felt that it was very important, as did Peter Bogdanovich, that the regional accents be accurate. Peter loved to talk to Orson Welles on the phone as often as possible, and Orson advised him to get a dialect coach. I had strong reservations about anybody from Los Angeles coming to Texas and creating an authentic Texas accent. My fear was that for one thing it would be too broad and secondly that it would be Southern and not Texan. Most of the Californians or New Yorkers that I've met could not distinguish between a Texas regional accent and a Southern one. The only one who struggled was Timothy Bottoms. And he was the only one that I think f—ed it up. Early in the movie, when he's making out with Charlene Duggs in the pickup truck, he's supposed to say, "Let's do somethin' different." And he refused to do that after many, many coaching sessions to tell him to say "somethin'"; he had to say "some*thang*." "Let's do some*thang* different." And it's in the movie, "some*thang*." It was one of those days I couldn't be on the set, and it snuck by me. And Peter didn't know the difference.

Bridges: When we were in Archer City there, shooting, somebody would nudge me and say, "Look, there's the real Duane." A lot of these characters were still walking around. All of us, the young guys especially, were fortunate to link up with a young fellow named Loyd Catlett. He was a young kid living in Wichita Falls at the time, and he was hired to play a part and to also coach us in dialect and just for us to observe and see what growing up in Texas was like. He was a wonderful help and a great friend to us all.

Platt: The hardest thing about making the movie was the climate, because we needed to shoot summer sequences and we got there in September. We started shooting in October, and we were desperate to get finished before Christmas. And we had to do the summer sequences in the coldest, freezingest—and only people in Texas know what I'm talking about, that wind coming down, right across the plains, flat, flat, flat. So the climate was hostile, and we had to have the kids in the movie—I was just a kid myself—but we had to have the kids in this little scanty clothing.

Leachman: When we were shooting in the main part of town, there was [a restaurant], I think it was called the Golden Rooster; we would always go in there, and while we'd be waiting, Ellen [Burstyn] and me, a woman we met at the restaurant would sit with us. And one day she was just beside herself. She finally burst into tears and said that she was married and everything, and we knew she was married anyway, and she was crying so uncontrollably. And we were consoling her and feeling very sorry, and she said, "No, not my husband; my lover." I mean, we were in the middle of *The Last Picture Show* without even realizing it.

THE CAST

Chason: Peter pretty much had Cybill in mind going in. He didn't really want to see anybody in Texas for the role of Jacy. However, I got him to agree to look at one actress in the state of Texas for that role, a girl from Dallas by the name of Patsy Calmes. I know the name Patsy Calmes doesn't ring any bells because Patsy moved to New York City and changed her name and got a job in soaps and is still working to this day. Now she lives in L.A., and the name that she changed her name to is "Morgan Fairchild."

Bogdanovich: Cybill was the only person I ever considered for the part. I saw her on the cover of *Glamour* magazine. I had never bought *Glamour* or even noticed it, but for some reason her expression on this one particular cover caught my attention in the supermarket, and I bought the thing and asked my assistant to find out who the girl was. And I went to New York and I thought she'd be perfect. She had a kind of offhand, destructive quality. I remember she came in to see me with her agent or her manager—I was at the Essex House, on Central Park South—and she came in wearing a Levi's jacket and Levi's jeans, a big girl. I had just had breakfast, and I was sitting on the couch with the coffee table in front of me and the remains of my breakfast—you know, sometimes they put a flower in a little vase, a little rose? So she sat on the floor on the other side of the coffee table, and we're talking, and she kind of offhandedly was fiddling with that little flower. And the way she did it, I thought, "Well, that's kind of the way she plays with guys, just kind of offhandedly." And that little gesture made me feel that she could do this part.

Platt: When I saw Cybill's picture—Peter leaves me out of this story—but I saw it and said to Peter, "Doesn't she look like Jacy?" We were shopping in the supermarket; he would never be in a supermarket without me. Well, it was interesting, because I had very high standards, and she was perfect. She had this sexual chip on her shoulder, certified, and I've never seen anybody who was more—she was gifted, a very gifted girl.

Bogdanovich: Polly had nothing at all to do with the casting of the movie. And of course I was in the supermarket alone. At that time in my life I chewed toothpicks, and I remember going to the supermarket on the way to the office to pick some up. Polly was already at the office, so she couldn't have been with me.

Shepherd: About the magazine cover and everything? I don't know who found it. What I always knew to be the case was Peter saw it in the grocery store and said, "Find this girl. That's Jacy." But now I've also heard that Polly says she found it. But, you know, who cares? It's like who designed Chartres.

S. Bottoms: I've always thought of Texas as my home away from home because I was, of course, discovered there, as an actor, and I've done some other work there. I never had a chicken-fried steak till I went to Texas. I never had a pecan pie till I went to Texas. I ate my first peanut pattie in Texas. A lot of firsts for me in Texas.

Bogdanovich: First day of shooting, as we were driving through town I saw this kid sitting on the steps; he was just sitting there, with his knees up, just sitting and watching. And I said, "Wait, stop the car, lemme get out a minute." And I went over and I said, "Who are you?" He said, "Well, I'm Sam Bottoms. I'm Tim's brother." I said, "Can you act?" He said, "Well, I don't know." I said, "You wanna be in the picture?" And he said, "Sure." He had braces all over his teeth, and I said, "Can you take your braces off?" And he said, "I don't know. I'll have to call my mom." And I said, "Well, go ahead, and if they let you do it, you can be in the picture." And that's how he got in the picture. He just looked right.

S. Bottoms: I didn't read the script. I didn't read the book. I didn't know what the story was about. I'd just come to work when they'd tell me to and I'd just stand where they'd tell me to. . . . Larry was real nice. He came out to the set. He paid me a nice compliment. He said, "I always kind of imagined Billy looked something like you."

Bogdanovich: Not only was John Ritter in the running [for the part of Sonny], he was the runner-up. His father came in to see me, with John—that's how I met Tex Ritter. I had met John, I liked him, and he read, I think, three or four times for the picture. Tex wanted to play Sam the Lion; he was sort of the runner-up for that. And he would have been good. I thought Ben was wonderful, though. Ben turned the picture down four times. I finally got John Ford to call him. Ford told him, "What are you gonna do, be Duke's sidekick the rest of your life?" Of course, Ben called me after that, and he said, "You put the old man on me." I said, "Ben, I really want you to do this." "Oh, Pete, I don't know," he said. "There's too many words in this picture. There's too many words." I told that to Ford, and he said, "Yeah, he always says there's too many words. He said there was too many words in *She Wore a Yellow Ribbon*. He just likes to ride." Finally, in the last meeting with him, I said, "Ben, you don't understand. If you do this picture, you're gonna get an Academy Award; you're gonna get a nomination at least." When I said it to him, he got angry. He said, "Why do you say that?" And I said, "Because I think so." "Goddammit," he said. "All right. I'll do the goddam thing."

SCENES

Bogdanovich: We were ready to shoot [the scene where Duane and Sonny are about to drive down to Mexico], and there was this line Ben's supposed to say—after [Sonny says,] "Oh, we're just gonna drink beer and tequila"—and he says, "Well, you catch the clap, you'll wish you hadn't drunk nothin'." And he says, "You, you, you—catch the miseries, you'll wish you hadn't drunk nothin'." And I said, "Cut. You catch the miseries— what the f—is that?" And he said, "I don't wanna say that other word." And I said, "Come on, Ben. What's miseries?" He said, "You know, like diarrhea." I said, "I don't know that anybody's gonna get that. Plus, it's not as funny as clap." And he said, "My mother might wanna see this picture, and I'm not gonna speak those dirty words." He wouldn't do it for about two takes, and I said, "Come on, say it with *clap*." And he said, "All right, god-dammit." So he said it. . . .

There were a lot of things we didn't plan. The most famous example for me was the scene by the tank dam when Ben has his big scene about the past, during which the sun came in and out about five times, really almost on cue. I mean, if somebody had asked me, "Where would you like the sun to come out and where would you like it to go back in again?"—it was absolutely extraordinary. It was the first take, which was a long piece of film. It was three or four minutes; there are some cuts in it now. And right toward the end of the scene, when the sun had done all these extraordinary things, the clouds and the sun, Tim Bottoms forgot one of his lines, and it was a long, like, twenty-five-, thirty-second pause, which effectively screwed up my notion that we wouldn't have a cut in it. And, well, I didn't know what to do. I mean, we got it, we printed that, and I said, "Let's do one more, to be safe." We did one more, and of course there was no pause but there were also no pirouettes from the sun, and anyway, there was no contest. I think Ben won the Oscar for that scene.

Chason: It fell to my department to find a photo double for Cybill [for the nude swimming party scene], somebody that was shaped like she was, and Peter wanted the actress, the photo double, to have tits that looked as much like Cybill's as possible. But Cybill would not allow a photograph or anything and wouldn't let me see them, so then she tries to describe to me in words what her tits look like. And they took a tape measure and measured and everything, and I went out looking for girls to double her. And I have to say it was not that unpleasant a task. I went to the talent agencies in Dallas, and they didn't blink an eye. They brought girls in and, you know, the girls would take off their tops and show their breasts. I wouldn't do the tape-measuring myself. We had a woman there, like a nurse.

But ultimately, if you look at how that scene was shot, it would have been extremely difficult to pull it off. Peter was able to talk Cybill into actually showing her breasts in the film and stripping down entirely, although you don't see anything below the waist.

Bogdanovich: The nude scenes were nervous-making. All of them. I didn't really want to shoot it that way, and the producers really wanted it that way, and I reluctantly did it. I was uncomfortable with it, but we did it. We had a lot of trouble finding an indoor swimming pool for that one scene; we just couldn't find one anywhere in Archer City or Wichita Falls. Finally somebody found one of those little kind of health spas in Wichita Falls, and we rented that. And we needed some kids who wouldn't mind getting stripped for the scene. And so we found some who agreed to do it, and I thought, you know, that I was going to be very delicate. All these kids, they came out buck naked; they didn't give a shit. And I was just looking up at the sky, saying, "Oh, shit." I was embarrassed; they weren't. Cybill and I were the only two who really didn't enjoy it. And those are the scenes that I'm still not that thrilled with.

Shepherd: I just recently looked at the movie, at his long version where he put the footage back in and he cut out one shot of my breasts. It's a funny, moving film that was very shocking and has more sex in it and more nudity than film today—you hardly see it anymore. And actually I ended up preferring, you know, like more nude scenes with me. You know, if you'd asked me—well, up until this last year, I would've probably said, "Oh, doing those nude scenes was so uncomfortable." But God, I look great. I—I would leave it all in there.

Leachman (on the scene in which her character first sleeps with Sonny): So the three of us got in the room together, this tiny little bedroom, Peter and Timothy and I, and the first thing out of anybody's mouth was Timothy saying, "I ain't taking off my clothes for this scene." So starting with that, we began to figure out how to do it. Each of us would go to a separate corner and undress down to our underwear, and then we would get into bed, but we wouldn't take off our underwear; another set of underwear was planted there. So Peter says, "Action," and we start taking off our clothes and we get into bed and he throws out his underwear, the plant, and I take off my bra and panties and throw them out. Completely. My character did it, I didn't. Of course we had to do it again; we couldn't stop laughing.

T. Bottoms: She was my mom's age. Sort of like being intimate with your mother. Very weird. And you know that Cybill Shepherd is just outside.

Bogdanovich: When I met Marlene Dietrich about a year and a half later—we were flying to Denver, and she was on the same plane with us, with Ryan O'Neal and me, and Ryan was bragging about me. And so he says, you know, "He directed *The Last Picture Show*. Didya see that?" And Marlene says, "Yes," and Ryan says, "What'd ya think?" And she says, "I thought if one more person strips slowly I vill scream." I must say I kind of understood what she meant, because that did make me a bit nervous; I thought there was an awful lot of sex in the picture.

Shepherd: Well, the first scene was very tough for me because of two reasons. I couldn't keep my eyes open 'cause it was very glary out by the lake. It was a love scene in the convertible with Tim Bottoms. Now, the first time I ever acted on-screen, I had to let this guy feel me up. He's very attractive, Timothy Bottoms, but frankly, I mean, I was not an experienced actress. The close-up—I think probably I look as good there as I ever looked on-screen. But it was kind of wild to be making out and have this guy feeling up my breasts, and of course we rehearsed quite a bit. And I tell you, we rehearsed. It was a very sexy thing, I mean, because Jeff Bridges is very attractive and very kind and very fun and Timothy Bottoms was, you know, very attractive and Peter Bogdanovich was very attractive. It was wild! It was just like—you didn't have to do drugs; the sexual thing of it was so, it was so exciting. I think I was aroused the whole entire shooting schedule, but don't let my mother read this article, 'cause she says, "All you do is talk about sex." Well, I don't care. I think that talkin' about sex is fun.

Bogdanovich (on the restored scene in which Jacy and Abilene, the oil-field foreman memorably played by Clu Gulager, have sex on the pool table): I had actually taken it out myself. Even now I'm not sure about it, but it's in there. It's an interesting scene, and it does help to explain Jacy's character a bit. It shows that she had an orgasm, and all that. At the time, I just thought it was too much about sex.

Chason (on the classroom scene in which the teacher is trying to interest the students in Keats's poetry): Bogdanovich wanted Sonny to look out the window and see some dogs screwing in the school yard. Well, the propman just threw his hands up in despair and refused even to try, said it couldn't be done, forget it. And that's what led Bogdanovich to say, "Well, I'll bet Gary Chason can do it." So I went to one of these old rancher guys and laid out my problem, and you know, it didn't take me any time, I was amazed. This ol' boy said, "Yeah, I got a bitch who's gonna be in heat next Saturday" — totally mysterious to me. But he knew. I mean, that's a man who really knew his dog. I said, "Okay, good. Do you have a male that she will mate with?" "Oh, yeah, a buddy of mine's got one." Those dogs cost me $25 a day; I mean, they were expensive. But then of course we weren't asking any of the other extras to do anything near like what we were asking the dogs to do.

Bogdanovich: When they voted at the school council on whether or not they'd let us shoot in there, we only got permission by one vote; it was that close. And they weren't happy with us at all when we shot that scene with the two dogs on the lawn of the school — we almost got thrown out of town for that one. Well, you can imagine what they thought — it's hard to imagine — but the camera was actually on the inside for that shot. You couldn't see the camera, you couldn't see anything except two huge lights outside lighting up these two dogs that are going at it. Just a few seconds; you don't actually see them do anything. You just see them sniffing around and the audience gets the idea; it gets a big laugh. But people driving by were horrified.

Chason: The propman had a long-standing relationship with Pabst Brewery, so the beer that the actors were going to drink in the movie was going to be Pabst Blue Ribbon. I said *no way,* and the propman was so pissed at me. I said, man, nobody in 1951 drank Pabst Blue Ribbon; it was unheard of here. It's gotta be Pearl and Lone Star; it can't be anything else. And so we're calling Pearl and Lone Star and getting labels and shit like that. You'll notice, though, we didn't have 'em in time for the big fight with Sonny and Duane over Jacy, when Duane hits him with the beer bottle. Jeff Bridges covered up the label because we didn't have the proper period labels yet.

Bogdanovich: One of those happy little accidents was Coca-Cola. There were several lines in the picture, "You wanna Coke?" And Columbia sent the script to the Coca-Cola Company—this was before Coke bought Columbia—and Coca-Cola said they didn't want to give us any product because they thought it was a dirty movie. That irritated me so much that I decided to remove not only any references to Coke but any casual shot in the background where you might see a Coke machine. And when I was down there researching, you know, getting ready, I noticed that a lot of people drank Dr Pepper. So I tried it—this was a regional drink; at the time, Dr Pepper was not known in the north—and I said, well, I'll just use Dr Pepper, and we changed the line to Dr Pepper; I thought it had more of an unusual sound anyway.

Chason: The town's name in the book is Thalia, but there was this town that had disappeared, called Anarene, and Peter thought that that sounded good, and so he wanted to name it Anarene. And we needed a school song because there's a time when they're driving in a car, in Jacy's convertible, and they sing it from beginning to end, at least in the director's cut. We needed lyrics, and so I ended up writing the lyrics to the school song.

Bogdanovich: There's one very nice scene that Larry always regretted wasn't in the original, which is early on in the picture when the three principal kids—Cybill, Tim, and Jeff—they get out of school and they jump into her car, and they're going to the place where they have the french fries. And before they get there, there's a scene where they're riding and Jeff imitates the coach and kind of spits like the coach, and kind of sarcastically they start to sing the school song. And they're sitting in the front seat, all of them singing the school song. I always regretted that we cut that. So that was one of the things we put back.

Chason: At the big graduation ceremony, for the state song they were gonna have "The Eyes of Texas." No, no, no, folks, "The Eyes of Texas" is the University of Texas song. The state song is called "Texas, Our Texas." I told Bogdanovich, and once he found out, he wanted authenticity, he wanted it to be real, so "Texas, Our Texas" is in the movie.

Bogdanovich: In the book, you know, it—the last picture show— was quite different. In the book it was a rather poor Audie Murphy movie, and I thought that the picture show ought to go out with a little bit more of a bang. You know, being a bit more romantic about the movies than Larry, who hates movies. He does. So I wanted to have a movie that had an adventure to it, some kind of movement, a trek of some kind. And there were really only two movies that I like—that fell within the range of directors that I like—and one was *Red River* and the other was John Ford's *Wagonmaster.* But because *Red River* is a Texas story—it starts in Texas and then they go north—and it was John Wayne, I thought it was more theatrical and more appropriate to the story, a bigger contrast between the adventurous past and the mundane present.

Bogdanovich: Life did intrude; my father passed away while we were shooting. Suddenly, of a stroke. And my marriage ended. And it couldn't have been more traumatic on a personal level. And yet, that's what movies are like. You just kind of keep going. So the present definitely intruded personally on our lives during the making of the film, but it was an obsessive—movies are an obsessive thing.

Shepherd: We were in Olney, Texas, and we were sitting in the theater—you know, 'cause the picture show in Archer City had burned down, we used the interior of Olney and the exterior we used in Archer City. So Peter and I are sitting in that theater, and we're talking and stuff, and I guess he knew that I was kinda having an affair with Jeff Bridges. And he said something—"Well, I guess you're lonely tonight"—and I said, "Oh, I'm lonely every night." And he said to me, "I can't decide who I'd rather sleep with, you or Jacy." I was very attracted to Peter. I knew he was a married man; I think I didn't have much of a conscience. I would try not to be involved with married men; I didn't think it was a great idea. It was very uncomfortable for all of us. But you know, looking back on it, would I do it differently? That's another question.

Platt: I was jealous, of course, wildly. I did Cybill's hair every day. I cut her hair, you know. I was tempted, but Cybill was irresistible. I thought about it—I thought if I was a man and a beautiful girl like that was making a pass at me, I don't know what I would do. I could see why Peter was so head over heels in love with her.

Brennan: I knew nothing of that. I had no idea it was going on. When we got home, I called Peter and said, "I want you and Polly to come to dinner." And he said, "Well, she won't be coming with me; better ask Polly separately." That's how I found out.

T. Bottoms: After work nobody really wanted to see anybody. Except Peter. He wanted to see what's-her-name. I think we all wanted to see her. Naked. I never saw her naked. I think Peter may have.

Bridges: The scenes with Cybill were very exciting to me; you use what's going on in your life. I was probably a little older than Duane was supposed to be, but all that—that young kind of feeling of sexual oats and all that stuff. Sure could call on that.

S. Bottoms: I was a youngster, so everybody kind of looked after me. I didn't get involved in a whole lot of the other stuff that was going on. I would actually have liked to. I didn't have a girlfriend then, but I was interested in what was going on after hours. It was pretty frustrating to a fifteen-year-old.

T. Bottoms: I really enjoyed Peter and Polly in the beginning, before we started shooting. But I know when Peter left Polly— she had just had a baby, I mean, a brand-new baby—and I don't know, I watched this beautiful marriage just destroyed. I watched it come apart, and it broke my heart, because at home my mom and dad were coming apart, so it was very personal, it just really hurt me, and I think that got reflected in my acting. Things just don't last—that's probably the worst feeling, a hopeless feeling, kind of like Sonny Crawford: hopeless despair.

S. Bottoms: It was painful to see all of this other stuff going on with all of these other people, in their lives. For me it was sort of a validation that everybody else's lives were pretty screwed up too and I wasn't the only one coming from a screwed-up background.

Bridges: We kind of had our own small town going; you know, you get very tight making a movie. It was almost like little incarnations, little lifetimes, and so there was like a bit of our own soap opera going there, and that was kind of like the life going on in the story.

Bogdanovich: The reason I wanted to shoot it in black and white is because I thought we would get a sense of the period better and more quickly. Period pictures in color are always troublesome, particularly if they're color at a time when there were movies. It's different if you're doing *Gone with the Wind,* 'cause there were no movies in that period. But when you're doing movies in a period that was essentially a black-and-white period, they're more realistic. Everything does seem more realistic in black and white, strange enough, even though it's an abstraction; it's one of those peculiarities. Also, I thought that the performances would resonate better. Orson Welles and I were talking about that, and I was telling him that I was trying to get something of what he did in terms of the depth of field in *Citizen Kane* or *The Magnificent Ambersons* or *Touch of Evil* and so on, and he said, "You'll never get it in color." And I said, "Well, what am I gonna do?" He said, "Shoot it in black and white." I said, "I don't think they'll let me." And he said, "Well, why don't you ask 'em?"

Leachman: I remember feeling that this picture, *The Last Picture Show,* it was as if—you've seen those books where you open the pages and the pages pop up and form things. That's what this seemed like; it just seemed like it just put itself up on the screen.

Platt: I think there are two huge, important things about that film. One is what we call the "environment," the atmosphere of the picture. The other was the fabulous nature of the material—great script, great land.

Bogdanovich: We had a hard time figuring out who was going to play Sam the Lion; we couldn't decide, and at one point people thought, well, what about Jimmy Stewart? We sort of thought about it, but I said, no, we really can't go all the way down there to the little town and end up with a movie star. And then Orson made a suggestion. He said, "How 'bout going down to Nashville; maybe you'll find some older, aging country singer that just might be perfect." So I did go to Nashville for that express reason, and while I was in Nashville I used the time to kind of do some research about country music of that period and found, to my amazement, that songs that I knew, like "Cold, Cold Heart," which I'd known as Tony Bennett's song, turned out to be originally a Hank Williams song. And I did a lot of research about the country hits during that period. The book is rather general about what years, it's very general in terms of the fifties. But I decided to be very specific, so the picture, as far as I was concerned, began in October 1951 and ended in October 1952, so I was very careful with that. A hit song in October 1951 on all the charts was Hank Williams's "Cold, Cold Heart." At the same time, Tony Bennett's version was popular in the north. So I decided to use mainly country music for the picture and the pop stuff more for Jacy, figuring that she was snobbish and didn't really like country music because it was too square as far as she was concerned.

Shepherd: One of my happiest memories was, oddly enough, getting up before light and riding out to work—to Archer City—and seeing that light. The light is so extraordinary! And that flat landscape makes the sky enormous. And I was just so thrilled to be going out, you know, and I think the whole crew—we all rode together—that was really fun. That's a more adventurous type of moviemaking than I've experienced since then.

Bridges: It was a very exciting time. Just making movies back in those days was very different. The movie was produced by a group of guys who had this company, bbs. bbs stood for Bert, Bob, and Steve. Any company that would give their first names as the company lets you know how loose creatively the company was. They produced *Easy Rider* and *Five Easy Pieces* and *The King of Marvin Gardens* and *The Last Picture Show* and some wonderful movies.

Brennan: To me it is a delicious, delicious memory. Camaraderie and all of that—and the time. Ten weeks. You know what they do now? Three. We would never be able to do that in three weeks. It's budgets.

Shepherd: When I got back to New York and I went back into modeling, I said, "I just had this incredible experience, making what I think could be a great movie." And everybody goes, "Well, who's in it?" And I listed the people, and nobody had ever heard of anyone in the film. I could see 'em click off—like, "Oh, yeah. Right."

S. Bottoms: If you ask my honest opinion, Tim's the movie. It's all coming from Sonny. I think Larry is Sonny. He doesn't want to admit it. Larry's Sonny, in an introverted, sort of twisted way. Shy.

Bogdanovich: I think *Picture Show* certainly had a tremendous impact and continues to have an impact. When you do something so meticulously within the period, you're dating it as you're making it. You're putting it in a time capsule. The ambience, the songs—everything is very much of that moment.

Bridges: I can recall after the first week of shooting, sitting around a table with Cloris Leachman and Ellen Burstyn and Cybill Shepherd, Eileen Brennan, and Tim was probably there, just the whole group of us, and we were having some breakfast together and we were all talking about—this is feeling very special, there's something kind of magical about this. So I remember having those feelings early on in the shooting, and I still have them today. I think *The Last Picture Show* really kind of stands alone. I can't think of any movie that it's like or is like it; it kinda sits there by itself.

1999

This was the first of three cover stories that I did for *Texas Monthly*, and Mary Ellen Mark's stylish photographs of the cast are a real bonus. I interviewed some of the actors by phone and visited in person with others involved in the making of the film. One thing I learned is that out-of-work actors answer their phone on the first ring and that to reach the stars—Jeff Bridges, Cybill Shepherd, Peter Bogdanovich— you have to go through several intermediaries before they'll talk to you. Almost everybody did talk, and everybody had pertinent things to say.

One of the standouts was Timothy Bottoms. I spent half a day with him in Santa Barbara, where he lives and where, at that time, he was working for his father installing aquatic sculptures. I interviewed Peter Bogdanovich by phone, and once he had our cell phone number he called several times to add information that he had forgotten to men- tion earlier. We would be driving around town and there was Peter on the phone. Later when I visited with Polly Platt in her office in Holly- wood, I began to understand the eternal debate between her and her former husband. At issue was who "owned" the creative artistry of the film. From a detached perspective, the film was truly a collabora- tive effort between them, but each wants full, if not total, credit. Polly had quit smoking, she told me, but reliving those days, she smoked half a pack in the hour and a half that we talked. Danny DeVito called, and they were going out to lunch. I had a late breakfast at a restaurant across the street and recognized George Clooney when he walked in to join a friend. That's the way it is out there; the stars are, as the tabloids say, just like us. Cybill Shepherd was a wonderful flirt on the phone. Gary Chasen, a production guy, was a great raconteur.

Nineteen years after making *The Last Picture Show*, Bogdanovich and most of the original cast returned to Archer City to film its sequel, *Texasville*. This time a star-struck town embraced the celebrities and welcomed the influx of fresh money into an oil-slump-depressed econ- omy. Several of the performers who had been young, unknown actors were now established figures: Cybill Shepherd, Jeff Bridges, Timothy Bottoms, Randy Quaid. The production had the air of a high school re- union. It also had, according to Timothy Bottoms, a noticeable class structure. The big stars lived in luxury trailers and the rest found housing in the town. Whereas the first film had an open set, this one was closed, and the whole town was far more movie-savvy than before. Only the French liked *Texasville*.

McMurtry continued to mine the characters and motifs of *The Last Picture Show,* writing three more sequels after *Texasville.* The best was *Duane's Depressed* (1999), a moving portrait of Duane Moore, ex-high school Lothario, successful oil man, and a man who, in late middle age, begins to discover much of what he has missed in his life, through a connection with nature and, oddly, Proust. It's one of McMurtry's best novels. It was followed by the increasingly thin and autumnal *When the Light Goes* (2007) and *Rhino Ranch* (2009). There may be nothing more to say about Thalia (Archer City) and environs, though in memoirs like *Walter Benjamin at the Dairy Queen* (1999) and *Paradise* (2000), one of my personal favorites, McMurtry found many vital and interesting things to tell us about his parents, Archer City, and Texas culture at the end of the twentieth century. In December of 2009 he published still another look back at his past, *Literary Life: A Second Memoir.*

As always, Larry is very hard on his own works. He writes in *Literary Life:* "Little of my work in fiction is pedestrian, but, on the other hand, none of it is really great. Maybe it will seem better to readers 50 years from now than it does to me today." I like Larry's hopefulness—that there will still be readers in 2059. Also, this gives me an opening to make a list, which I always enjoy doing. Here, in my considered opinion, are the essential works of fiction authored by Larry Jeff McMurtry: *Horseman, Pass By; Leaving Cheyenne; The Last Picture Show; Moving On; All My Friends Are Going to Be Strangers; Lonesome Dove;* and *Duane's Depressed.* (McMurtry, incidentally, in his new memoir rates *Duane's Depressed* as his best novel.) Then there are the essential nonfiction works like *In a Narrow Grave: Essays on Texas* (which also happens to be great); the Walter Benjamin book; *Paradise;* and perhaps, taken in bits, the three volumes of memoirs—*Books* and *Literary Life,* plus the remaining one, on Hollywood, to be published in due course—and you have a very significant body of work. Others will have their own favorites and can add to or amend my list, but that is part of the pleasure of making lists and checking them twice.

DONNIE DOES *DALLAS*

Even now, twenty-odd years from the end of the TV phenomenon known as *Dallas,* 300,000 pilgrims a year journey to the legendary site of Southfork in southwest Collin County. They want to see the ranch, they want to pay homage. They visit the small *Dallas* museum there, and they take the tour. All of this is fascinating to me, but not, I must say, to everybody. Recently I was at a gathering of academics (or accas as the Aussies call them), and for some reason the subject of that old eighties TV show came up. The accas were uniformly proud not to have seen a single episode. Not me. I was a big fan then, and now in the long aftermath of the last, the final show, I am still intrigued.

Dallas, you have to remember, was everywhere. Reruns ran in ninety countries around the globe; it was hard to escape. When we flew from Dallas (the city) in 1994 to Dominica, the little, obscure, off-the-tourist-track island in the Lesser Antilles where Jean Rhys was born and raised, *Dallas* was there waiting for us, flickering on tiny TV screens in houses open to the warm tropical nights. At a literary conference in Sydney, Australia, in the late nineties, a Turkish woman interviewed me on Turkish radio, and all she wanted to talk about was *Dallas.* The show was gold; it was international currency.

Dallas occurred at a propitious moment in the history of Texas, in the midst of but also near the last phase of the last oil boom in the state. Things on the cultural front were booming too. Between 1978 and 1980 two familiar character types were reconfigured and recycled: the drugstore cowboy and the wheeler-dealer oil man. The new and improved drugstore cowboy, created by Aaron Latham in his 1978 *Esquire* article, "The Ballad of the Urban Cowboy: America's Search for True Grit," made it to the silver screen in 1980, and the film *Urban Cowboy* set off a virulent but short-lived craze for wearing cowboy duds and riding mechanical bulls. Although the urban cowboy spent his nights dancing at Gilley's, he spent his days working in the petrochemical refineries of Houston. The urban cowboy was the blue-collar bottom rung of the oil empire presided over, in popular culture, by that second incarnation of a familiar Texas archetype, J.R. Ewing, the beloved and much hated oilman/wheeler-dealer of the glitzy TV melodrama, *Dallas*.

J.R. derived in part from James Garner's comic portrayal of a Texas oilman in *The Wheeler Dealers,* a winning comedy that had the misfortune to premiere in Dallas on November 20, 1963, just two days before Texans were no longer loveable good ol' boys. (A minor wheeler-dealer in the film is named J.R., by the way. The character also owed something to James Dean's wildcatter of *Giant. Dallas* hit TV screens in 1978 and by 1980 had become part of the lexicon of the nation and the world. The show's impact would prove to be global.

And it all appears something of an accident, how *Dallas* came into being in the first place. Most of the facts are recounted in Suzy Kalter's *The Complete Book of* Dallas: *Behind the Scenes at the World's Favorite Television Show* (1986), an indispensable source for *Dallas* lore.

The genesis of *Dallas* begins in 1977, when a writer named David Jacobs was trying to put together a new show for Lorimar Productions. Jacobs wanted to write a series to be called *Knots Landing,* which would deal with four families, but he couldn't sell it to the executives. They wanted something with a little more glamour and they wanted Linda Evans to star in it. So Jacobs started working on a story with the catchy title of "Untitled Linda Evans Project." Jacobs himself credits another person, Richard Berger, at that time a CBS executive, with coming up with the idea of Dallas. Berger had the notion that the Southwest had been underrepresented in TV drama land, and besides that, he was reading Tommy Thompson's *Blood and Money* at the time. (So why didn't they call it *Houston?*)

Across the nation, in popular culture media, Dallas the city, the word, was undergoing a kind of rehabilitation after more than a decade of being tagged with all the negative associations of the Kennedy assassination. The Dallas Cowboys team was a big factor; so were the Dallas Cowboy Cheerleaders, including a made-for-TV movie of the same title, in 1979. Pete Gent's novel *North Dallas Forty* enjoyed national success. Dallas was recovering from its Kennedy hangover.

The suggestion to situate the story in Texas suited Jacobs. Although he had himself never been to Texas, he had once dated a girl from Waco. On the day Jacobs's partner, Michael Filerman, and Jacobs were to present their project to the network honchos, Filerman said he wasn't going into a meeting to pitch something called "Untitled Linda Evans Project"; it didn't have enough class. So he wrote "Dallas" on the cover sheet, pointing out that it could always be changed later. Of such casual, improvisational decisions is cultural history made. Linda Evans, by the way, was not going to work out anyway; originally Jacobs intended the part of Pam for her but it became clear that the role was too small to accommodate a star of Evans's magnitude; she needed something bigger, something like *Dynasty*.

CBS wanted a "saga" and everybody now agreed that "modern, urban Texas" was saga country. Leonard Katzman, the producer, commented on the Texas aura: "Texas has always had kind of a mythic quality about it. Dallas was the place that everybody knew. It just seemed like that was a grabber by itself initially, just the name." Jacobs said much the same thing: "Texas is just one of those trigger words that, to me, suggests big scale, big spaces." Here again is how he describes his conception of Texas, though I think it bears repeating that at that point he had never been to the state: "Bigger, brasher, richer, newer than the Northeast, not so trendy as California. A setting that matched Wall Street in the harboring of unfathomable wealth, and equaled Tennessee Williams's South in the fostering of unrelenting decadence."

"But where in urban Texas?" he continues. "Houston, maybe? No, too modern for a saga, too new and oil rich, deep dark secrets can't be hidden behind all those glass walls. San Antonio? Too exotic, almost Mexican. Austin? Fort Worth? Waxahachie?"

No, the only place, the inevitable place, was Dallas. Says Jacobs, "I may have blanched when I realized I was setting a television show in the town where Kennedy had been killed, but on reflection I decided that fifteen years was long enough to hold the grudge; besides, the Dallas Cowboys had won the Super Bowl the year before and that somehow entitled the city to a fresh start." So it would be Dallas, not Houston. Houston he thought of as more like Atlanta, but Dallas, for him, had "those connotations of the Old West."

Again, without any firsthand knowledge, Jacobs's imagination envisioned the city of Dallas as an "arena for saga, at once a big city and a redneck town, a place with right and wrong sides of the track—one side populated by barefoot bumpkins and the other side by millionaire bumpkins." It's the *barefoot* that gives one pause, those of us who have been to Dallas.

Jacobs, like a latter-day Whitman afoot with his vision, explains his soaring conception: "So I went to work on *Dallas,* evoking as best I could the texture and character of this great booming metropolis where cowboys crossed paths with oilmen in the shadow of towers built by financial men, where Old West and Central Sunbelt met to form what might be New America. It felt right to me; I could feel the grit between my fingers."

At this point Jacobs came up with the radical idea that he ought to *go* to Dallas, but his partner persuaded him against it. No need to go to Dallas until *after* CBS buys the script, he advised Jacobs. Jacobs completed his first draft of *Dallas* on December 10, 1977. Six weeks later he and the cast and crew were in Dallas to film five episodes. *Dallas,* by the way, did not start out as a series but as independent hour-long dramas that were meant to create an audience for a series, and that is what happened.

On the ground in Dallas, the city Jacobs had *invented,* the author, the visionary, said that he didn't have to change much. Location shooting was important chiefly because the producers wanted to get away from an L.A. look with ubiquitous palm trees in every shot.

When Jacobs talks about *Dallas,* what he stresses most is conflict and structure of the story line; conflict is what spurs viewer interest; all the rest is background. The details about a real place named Dallas are unimportant. Thus in one early episode a hurricane strikes Dallas, but nobody cared that this would not happen in real life. Just as nobody cared that oil has never been found in Dallas County. These are minor factors when compared with the power of story, of narrative conflict and audience engagement. In *Dallas* the "inciting incident"—the narrative event that generates everything—takes place before the first episode. The whole idea of *Dallas* starts not with J.R. Ewing, as anybody might think, but with Pamela Barnes Ewing. Jacobs began with Pamela, not J.R.: "The idea was that a poor girl from the wrong side of the tracks marries into a rich Texas oil family." As Jacobs defines it, "the inciting incident in *Dallas* occurs when Bobby Ewing marries Pamela Barnes. Boy has met girl, married her in a quickie ceremony in New Orleans, and is now taking her home to live happily ever after with his family, pretending that fifty years of animosity between the Ewings and the Barneses will not affect their relationship."

In Jacobs's analysis, *Dallas* begins with the complicating incident, not the inciting incident. And the complicating incident can be stated in one line of dialogue, uttered by Pamela, Bobby's new bride: "Your family's gonna throw me off the ranch." Meaning, in actual practice, Bobby's brother, J.R. In the early days, though, J.R. and the actor who would make him a household name, Larry Hagman, did not count for much. When the first episode of *Dallas* started filming in the city, the *Dallas Morning News* did not even mention Larry Hagman. In the beginning Patrick Duffy was the biggest star in the production, but Larry Hagman, with his infectious enthusiasm for the role of J.R., quickly put his stamp on the show. Hagman, incidentally, has recently talked about where he got his conception of the J.R. type. According to Hagman, the inspiration came from a Texas businessman in Weatherford, Texas, where the young Hagman spent a year when he was a teenager. (His mother, Mary Martin, was from Weatherford.) In an interview in 2009 Hagman recalled the origins of the character J.R.: "I worked for this guy named Jess Hall Jr., and I learned all about J.R. right there from him. How to be fun and have a good time. How to be ruthless." The first five episodes ran on consecutive Sunday nights beginning on April 2, 1978. The first show was called "Digger's Daughter."

Episode number 4, "Winds of Vengeance," is one of my favorites. This is the one where a hurricane threatens Dallas and most of the men folk leave Southfork to deal with the storm. (Here of course is another instance when the geography of Texas is of little consequence to writers and producers. The real city of Dallas has been hit by tornadoes, but any hurricane that hits Dallas is going to be the mother of all hurricanes.) Left behind are J.R. and Ray Krebbs, who are forced to watch while Luther Frick (rhymes with . . .), played by Brian Dennehy, gets revenge on J.R. for shacking up with his wife in a Waco motel. Luther Frick makes Sue Ellen dress up in her Miss Texas swimsuit and sing, in that quavering, lip-trembling style that Linda Grey specialized in, "People Who Love People Are the Luckiest People in the World." Prime-time soap doesn't get much better than this.

From those early episodes, *Dallas* gathered to a greatness. The peak of audience interest occurred fairly early, on November 21, 1980, when the episode "Who Shot J.R.?" aired. Fifty-seven countries tuned in, 350 million people watched, and Jimmy the Greek—remember him?—laid odds correctly on his favorite, Sue Ellen's sister Kristen. In the Sesquicentennial year—remember that?—1986, *Texas Monthly* listed the "Who Shot J.R.?" show as one of the 150 most important events in the history of the Lone Star State. Maybe so.

The stats about *Dallas* are worth a brief doffing of one's Stetson. The show ran for over a decade, from April 2, 1978 to May 3, 1991. It was the top-rated program on TV in 1980–1981 and 1981–1982, second in 1982–1983, number one again in 1983–1984, and number two in 1984–1985. It spawned a host of sudsy prime-time imitators, including, of course, Jacobs's first love, *Knots Landing*. J.R. became more than a household name; he became a product; there were J.R. buttons, T-shirts, a brand of blue jeans, a beer called J.R.'s Private Stock. A rock group in England released a record; on one side, a song called "I Love J.R."; on the other, "I Hate J.R." (Steven Reddicliffe's 1988 *Texas Monthly* article, "Is J.R. Shot?" is crammed with such desiderata.)

There were other, seedier indicators of *Dallas*'s influence. One of the best-known porno flicks of the era was called *Debbie Does Dallas* (1978), featuring the sexual escapades of a cheerleader in a locker room setting. In *The Dallas Schoolgirls* (1981) the connection with *Dallas* was explicit, as was the sex. In an early scene a Stetson-wearing J.R. Ewing type received oral sex as his private plane descended into Dallas. Sample dialogue: "I'm gonna shoot like an oil well." Another quadruple X-er of 1981, *Wild Dallas Honey,* also capitalized on the *Dallas* title.

The saturation and pervasiveness of a phenomenon like *Dallas* in popular culture tends to produce broader cultural analyses to try to account for a show's dominance and popularity.

The first theory is based entirely on second-hand hearsay. According to the views of some writers and directors, the show, especially the character of J.R., was largely a reflection of producer Leonard Katzman's psyche. There is a documentary about the making of *Dallas* that is floating around on cable TV that I have not yet been able to see. According to what I have been told, some of the writers interviewed for the documentary cite Katzman's personality as the driving force behind their conception of J.R. Katzman apparently was a flamboyant type who loved the perks of Hollywood success and relished flash, glitz, and power. So that is one thesis that has absolutely nothing to do with Texas and everything to do with Leonard Katzman. Those qualities, incidentally, would not seem to make Katzman unique in TV/Movie Land.

James Walcott offered up another theory in a commentary on the deeper, extra-textual meanings of *Dallas,* written for *Texas Monthly*'s Sesquicentennial issue of January 1986. According to Wolcott, the appeal of *Dallas* is rooted in the JFK family saga. Especially the episode "Who Shot J.R.?" Walcott notes the significance of the date when this segment aired: November 21, reminding everybody, not so subtly, of November 22, that other day when a shooting took place in Dallas and of all the questions attendant upon who shot JFK. That J.R.'s brother is named Bobby is not lost on Walcott. Here is Walcott laying out his premise for a Kennedy matrix to the "Who Shot J.R.?" episode: "Once again, the world was absorbed by the spectacle of violence in Dallas, and once again the climate of the town was partially to blame, except that the reprehensible atmosphere of hate of 1963 had evolved into the glamorized business ethos of 1980."

I find that I have said little about oil itself as the economic foundation of the Ewing empire. This seems to me self-evident. It has always seemed to me that in *Dallas* the cattle were just there as props, as yard art. In Texas movies, generally, oil trumps cattle, but the cattle are good for nostalgic and ethical value. They bespeak an older, better time when men carved out an empire rather than gambled their way into wealth. The line of succession in the cattle-vs-oil paradigm runs from *Giant* through *Hud* and *The Last Picture Show* to *Dallas.* Since *Dallas* and *Urban Cowboy,* there has been no signature popular culture expropriation of Texas that comes anywhere close to the phenomenal popularity and long-running success of *Dallas*—with one huge exception, the miniseries *Lonesome Dove,* and that compelling saga was a study in inspired nostalgia, a post-Sesquicentennial throwback to pre-oil Texas. It was all about cattle. *Friday Night Lights,* the much praised "artistic" TV drama series, has its followers but has no mythic dimensions or national impact.

Is there likely to be anything that will match *Dallas* in the future? Hard to say, but personally, I find it difficult to imagine a new David Jacobs trying to pitch a melodrama about the wind-powered sources for electricity going online in the dusty reaches of West Texas. Somehow the story of a lusty family that makes a fortune out of wind turbines and solar energy and drives around in electric minicars and worries a lot about carbon footprints—it just doesn't have that larger-than-life Lone Star élan.

2001

In the *plus ça change* category, it is amusing to see that a new Texas-themed TV soap is springing from that very West Texas soil that I was so skeptical about in the closing remarks of this essay. *Lonestar* it's called, and according to *The Hollywood Reporter,* we can look forward to "a subversive soap that follows a polygamist juggling two very different lives and two wives, set against the backdrop of the greed and corruption of Texas oil and power industries." Another character from the new show sounds very familiar too: "a gravelly voiced titan at home in boots or a three-piece suit." *Plus ça change, plus c'est la même chose.*

BROKEBACK
MOUNTAIN IN MY
REARVIEW MIRROR

The last time I saw Larry was in his domicile in Archer City, back in 2002. The occasion was the thirtieth anniversary of Peter Bogdanovich's film *The Last Picture Show,* based on Larry's novel. (The celebration had been delayed a year because of 9/11). On Friday afternoon, before the public program on the following day, Larry hosted a small reception at his imposing home, a prairie-style three-story house that was once the country club for the little golf course that lies just beyond the periphery of Larry's yard. Walking up to the impressive door, I felt like Benjy Compson standing near the fence watching the men striking the white balls, while inside the mansion Larry Compson McMurtry counted his money.

The guests that day were glittering. Besides my beautiful wife, Betsy Berry, and myself, there were Jeff Bridges and his sidekick double, Loyd Catlett, a local boy from Wichita Falls who upon landing a small part in *The Last Picture Show* had caught a terminal case of Hollywood fever. He'd moved to L.A. after Bogdanovich's company packed up and left, back in '70, and was there still, making a living working as Jeff Bridges's double in over forty films. Jeff and Loyd were good company that weekend. And Cloris Leachman was present. Cloris, it turns out, has a diva's self-regard. She spent the entire afternoon begging Larry to write her a part in something, in anything. Perhaps *Loop Group* was conceived that day.

There were many lasting impressions—Larry's warm hospitality; Larry's Hermes 3000 typewriter (later to be memorialized in his Golden Globes acceptance speech as "one of the noblest instruments of European genius"); Larry's stacks of manuscript pages awaiting their turn in his assembly line of forthcoming books; Larry's deep affection for his grandson, "Master Curtis," who was staying with him that weekend; Larry's library of books about rivers—thousands of them line the walls of one of the huge, high-ceilinged rooms on the first floor. But one offhand literary remark resonates to this day—Larry mentioning a story that he had read that he considered—I still remember the exact phrase—a "small masterpiece." That story was Annie Proulx's "Brokeback Mountain."

I didn't think anything more about it until I read somewhere that Larry and Dianna Ossana, who was not there the afternoon of the soiree, were involved in making a film from said story, and the rest is history—Larry in tuxedo jacket and jeans, Dianna in traditional Oscar garb at the Academy Awards, both clearly enjoying their moment of Hollywood love.

Eventually I went to see the film before it left the big screen—I wanted to get the beauty of it hot—and there were some things about it that I liked a great deal: chiefly the landscapes in Wyoming (actually Alberta, Canada), and some of the cowboys' hard-bitten mannerisms, especially Heath Ledger's slit-lipped taciturnity. (Ledger was a natural for classic Westerns, as evidenced by his performance in the Australian Western, *Ned Kelly*). But what I didn't like much is what I hadn't liked in Westerns when I was a kid, and that was all the kissing and stuff that just slowed down all the shootin' and horse ridin'. I didn't mind it so much in Gene Autry films because instead of kissing, he'd sing a song, and that's one of the things I missed in *Brokeback Mountain:* I missed the singing.

The presence of Eros in Westerns has always been a dodgy business, to my mind, and so I found all the male-to-male romance about as irritating as the parry and thrust between male and female in all the old Westerns. And all the time, I was thinking, what about the sheep? Here was an ancient option, going back to classical Greek pastoral, but, unfortunately, the film was silent on this subject. Although there is one moment, early in the proceedings, when a scalded-looking Randy Quaid tells the two cowboys that every night one of them must "sleep with the sheep." This is not coded language; it does not have a prurient content, the way I was hoping it would. It means to sleep with the sheep, not heh heh *sleep* with the sheep.

The most famous line in the film and the one I saw quoted the most, in advert clips on TV, is the one that I am now going deliberately to misquote: "I wish I knew how to quirt you." *Quit* of course is what Jack Twist, one of the coyboy lovers, says to the other, Ennis del Mar. (Incidentally, one has to admire the names; so very Dickensian: Twist(ed); and Ennis . . . of the Sea.) But wouldn't it have been much better, much tastier, much more au courant, for the verb to be *quirt*?

The fact is, S&M has often found a home on the range. In the only film Marlon Brando ever directed, the estimable *One-Eyed Jacks,* Karl Malden smashes Brando's hands with a rifle butt, repeatedly, brutally, and Brando seems at some level to enjoy it. The scene goes on forever, and it takes him a lot of screen time to recover. This is but one example. In *The Man from Laramie* Jimmy Stewart is forced to extend his open palm, the palm of peace, the vulnerable flesh where they nailed poor, suffering Jesus, to a rancher's possibly gay son, who fires a bullet through the hand. Yowsa. And then there's Lash Larue, a B-movie icon who dressed in black leather and used a whip instead of a six-gun to tame the West. He was king of the quirters. And what about *The Gay Caballero,* which was so good it was filmed thrice, in 1929, 1932, and again in 1940. It might be time to film that sucker again.

All the sex in *Brokeback Mountain* is from the source, Annie Proulx's story. But my argument with the story is not about sex but about how people talk. Proulx has some serious trouble with how Westerners speak.

The abuse of Western/Texan speech in "Brokeback Mountain" is extensive, a fact I was a bit surprised to find when I finally got round to reading it. After all, you wouldn't expect to find a flaw in a story that Larry calls "a great story" and a "literary masterpiece." In a little three-page essay, "Adapting Brokeback Mountain," Larry, in fact, praises "the struggling, bruised speech still to be heard today across the north plains." This essay appears in a useful book titled *Brokeback Mountain: Story to Screenplay,* a spin-off volume containing essays by McMurtry, Proulx, and Ossana, plus the text of the story and the screenplay. Altogether it offers kind of complete one-stop shopping for the whole phenomenon of Brokebackiana.

According to Proulx (whose name derives from the Latin *prolix*), the story went through sixty (60) drafts before she was satisfied. But a feeling persists that it might have taken sixty-one (61) to get it right. In any case here are some examples from this "literary masterpiece" of how cowboys talk, using the *a* word:

> "You been a Mexico, Jack?"
> "You used a come away easy."

And this:

> "Christ, it got a be all that time a yours ahorseback makes it so goddamn good. We got to talk about this. Swear to god I didn't know we was goin a get into this again . . ."
> "We got a work out what the fuck we're goin a do now."

This *a* tic runs all the way through the story, and it's a tiring a read it. Proulx's weird Western dialect is apparently catching, like a low-grade infection. A prime example is Kent Meyers's South Dakota novel, *The Work of Wolves* (2004). Of the three main characters in this novel, the Native American speaks perfect English, the German exchange student speaks imperfect, German-inflected English, and the third, an Anglo cowboy, suffers from the same a-ffliction as Proulx's lonesome cowboys. It's a mystery why this is a happening.

At one point Proulx mentions specifically the Texas way that Jack Twist talks: "A little Texas accent flavored his sentences, 'cow' twisted into 'kyow' [but then his name is Twist, remember] and 'wife' coming out as 'waf.'" Surely only characters on *Hee Haw* ever talked this way.

I don't think it's insignificant that this story was published in the *New Yorker.* (*Harper's,* incidentally, passed on publishing the story.) The fiction editor up there at the *New Yorker* doesn't know a cow from a cow pattie. I am sure of this because I've seen her in action. She came down to Austin a couple of years ago and made it clear to everybody that she and her *New Yorker* cohorts had traveled, in coming to Texas, deep into the deepest of the fartherest, most remote, most godforsaken boonies, far beyond the pale of haute civilization. Not even Austin's blue state standing could redeem the sheer bewilderment and horror with which she confronted this distant and provincial place, this heart of darkness, this desert of the beaux arts.

I adduce one more example, from another recent *New Yorker* story titled "Cowboy," by Thomas McGuane. In it the vernacular narrator says sumbitch and that oldsumbitch in virtually every sentence. McGuane, a Westerner, ought to know better. But outsiders don't have a clue. A novelist from England who lives in New York came to the University of Texas for a visiting-writer stint, and one of the things he did was to xerox "Cowboy" for his students to read because he thought it spoke their language. I personally have never heard sumbitch used except by some loser telling some lame joke. But son of a bitch, that's a different matter. I use it daily driving the clogged arteries of the capitol of the Lone Star State, rolling out the phrase in all its plangent richness: YOU SON OF A BITCH. But not sumbitch, never. Go back to New York City, I do believe I've heard enough.

In "From Adapting *Brokeback Mountain*" Larry gives all the credit to Proulx for discovering and writing about a part of Western experience that had been ignored until Annie got her gun: "I was the more stunned when I read 'Brokeback Mountain' because I realized that it was a story that had been sitting there all my life, fifty-five years of which have been lived in the American West. There the story was, all those years, waiting in patient distance for someone to write it." Proulx herself has commented on the origins of her insight into homosexual cowboys. In "Getting Movied" she describes a scene that she witnessed in a bar in Wyoming. An older cowboy was watching some younger cowboys shoot pool, and Proulx was watching him. She explains, "Maybe he was following the game, maybe he knew the players, maybe one was his son or nephew, but there was something in his expression, a kind of bitter longing, that made me wonder if he was country gay." And this is evidence? Maybe they engaged in a secret handshake. *Maybe?* This is the crux of her invention of a Gay Cowboy West? For the record, I have no doubt that there were gay cowboys. A couple of years ago an RTF graduate student at UT, Jessica Dorfman, asked me to serve as an on-camera commentator in a film she was making about gay rodeo cowboys and I did so. It was fun. We talked, among other things, about the scene in *Red River* where one cowboy admires the size of another's pistol with plenty of double entendres thrown in to make the scene completely "gay." *Cowboys to Me* can be viewed online under that title.

What's odd about McMurtry's sense of having missed a gay reality in the West is that McMurtry hadn't missed it at all; he had already written about it, as we shall see. Whether Larry forgot or misremembered, I don't know.

In Larry's second novel, *Leaving Cheyenne,* published in 1963, he included a gay subtext. Of course Larry has dismissed this work, as he has others of his early novels. He now considers *Leaving Cheyenne* naïve because it is based on the jejune view that two cowboys could sexually love the same woman for all their lives without killing each other. According to Larry, journalists of his acquaintance love this novel because it matches their own self-delusions about sharing the same woman in a kind of no-fault triangle.

This story of two cowboys in love with the same woman is a triangulation of Leslie Fiedler's buddy theory of homoerotic American heroes as laid out in his famous book, *Love and Death in the American Novel.* Fiedler made it a condition of his theory that there had to be a racial bifurcation as well; thus the paradigmatic types are Hawkeye and Chingochkook (Chicago in Mark Twain's pastiche), Ishmael and Queequeg, Huck and Jim, Randall

McMurphy and Chief Bromden, and I would add, Crockett and Tubbs in *Miami Vice,* just to bring us more up to date. One might ask why can't the two homoerotic figures be of the same race? The answer to this is, I don't know.

In *Leaving Cheyenne* the beloved Molly has a son by each cowboy, and one of the sons, Jimmy, turns out to be gay. Jimmy goes to fight in World War II, and in the last letter he sends his mom he tells her about his new way of being:

> Don't worry, I am not going to marry no girl, Filipino or otherwise. I'm not very religious no more, this war has caused that, and I don't take after girls any more, I take after men. I have a friend who is rich, and I mean rich, he says if I will stay with him I will never have to work a day, so I am going to. I guess we will live in Los Angeles if we don't get killed.

Here McMurtry shows considerable understanding of Jimmy's existential condition, although it is odd that in his new book, *Literary Life: A Second Memoir,* Larry characterizes Jimmy as "Molly's cruel gay son."

An even more interesting possible connection between *Leaving Cheyenne* and Proulx's story is the use of the verb *quit* at a key moment in the novel.

Running across four pages of text, the word *quit* dominates the discourse when Gid, the sternest of the two cowboy lovers, tells Molly that he is not going to have sex with her any more. I wish I could quit quoting but I can't:

> And Gid was going to quit me.
>   Please don't quit me, Gid.
>   You quitting me won't make nothing up to him.
>   Molly, it ain't quitting. . . . I never quit nothing in my life.
>   Right after he had quit me . . .
>   . . . he had suffered so much to quit doing.

If he really wanted to quit that bad . . .
For a month or so after Gid quit me . . .
Now that you've quit [all that's left is a band of
gold . . .]

So when Larry read "Brokeback Mountain," he would have
been very familiar with the emotional terrain and with the word
quit to express loss, sadness, the irresistible tug of love in all its
forms. But surely he could not have foreseen the pop cult per-
sistence of *quit,* for it looks as though the line from the film may
enjoy a long shelf life. According to the *Daily Texan,* the student
newspaper at the University of Texas, in the months following
the movie's peak in popularity, the phrase can't-quit-you became
enshrined in undergraduate college culture as the "punch line
of bad college jokes." It's in commerce, too. A high-end grocery
store in Austin sells a product called Cowboy Soap. Its ingredi-
ents include apricot seeds, beer, and avocado oil. Cowboy Soap
is designed to "help keep your Cowboy or Cowgirl skin soft and
touchable." The slogan? YOU JUST CAIN'T QUIT THIS SOAP.
   So too does the culture seem unable to quit *Brokeback Mountain.* It turns up in British novelist Sebastian Faulks's 2007
novel, *Engleby,* as a marker of strangeness: "It's 7 March, 2006,
and I understand that a film about gay cowboys has just won
an Oscar." (The speaker has been confined to a mental institu-
tion for eighteen years.) In the satirical British film *In the Loop,*
a character speaks of another's sexual proclivities and wonders
whether he has had a "Brokeback moment." Robin Williams
routinely uses the phrase "Brokeback moment" in his comedy
routines. The same phrase appears in a poem, "Split Seconds,"
published in an avant-garde literary periodical, *Court Green,* in
2009. Poet R. Zamora Linmark writes, "Keoni just gave me my
Brokeback-Mountain-moment/Minus-the-slaughtered-sheep-
on-the-pasture for the day/What do you mean I tripping up
on my fantasies?" Then there's the thirty-second Bun-o-Vision
which shrink-wraps the entire plot to half a minute, "re-enacted
by bunnies." A true work of genius, it won a 2008 Webby Award.
(The Web site is www.angryalien.com/aa/brokebackbuns/asp.)

And *Brokeback* pops up in the sports world, too. In November 2007, after a loss to the San Antonio Spurs, Coach Phil Jackson of the Los Angeles Lakers explained to the press: "We call this a 'Brokeback Mountain' game because there's so much penetration and kickouts. It was one of those games." The NBA made him issue a formal apology: "If I've offended any horses, Texans, cowboys, or gays, I apologize."

2009

I gave a version of this talk at a literary conference held at Texas A&M University. The audience, mostly students, seemed to like it, though the organizer of the conference, an academic, seemed not to. It will be interesting to see how long this film keeps reverberating through the culture.

The latest incarnation of a Brokeback comedy moment can be seen in a bit of satire inspired by Tiger Woods's amorous misadventures. A mock movie poster of *Broke Black Golfer* surfaced on the Internet in spring 2010. It depicts Tiger wearing a denim jacket and a cowboy hat pulled low over his eyes while next to him stands a blonde cowgirl, the two parodying the movie poster poses of the stars of *Brokeback Mountain*. The supporting cast consists of "Elin Nordegren-Woods and lots of other chicks." The ad tagline is: "Love is a bitch—times 11."

BIBLIOGRAPHY

Articles, Books, and Interviews by
Don Graham on Texas Literature, Film,
History, and Culture from 1999 to 2009

1999

"Proust in Texas: Larry McMurtry's Rebel Without a Car." *The Texas Observer* 91.11 (January 22, 1999), 32–33.

"Picture Perfect: The Making of *The Last Picture Show*" [cover story]. *Texas Monthly*, February 1999, 72–80, 106–111.

"Cotton Tale." *Texas Monthly*, May 1999, 108, 110,114, 116.

"Larry McMurtry's Texas-sized Career." *The Texas Writer* 1.1 (May 1999), 3–6.

"Don Graham's Texas Classics: *Horseman, Pass By.*" *Texas Monthly*, June 1999, 24.

"Don Graham's Texas Classics: *The Gay Place.*" *Texas Monthly*, July 1999, 26.

"Perspectives on McMurtryville: A Memoir by Archer City's Flaubert." *Texas Observer* 91.13 (July 23, 1999), 5–7.

"Don Graham's Texas Classics: *Pale Horse, Pale Rider.*" *Texas Monthly*, August 1999, 28.

"Teaching Texas Fiction." *English in Texas* 29.2 (Fall/Winter 1999), 21–23.

"Don Graham's Texas Classics: *North Towards Home.*" *Texas Monthly*, September 1999, 30.

"Don Graham's Texas Classics: *Some Part of Myself.*" *Texas Monthly*, October 1999, 24.

"Don Graham's Texas Classics: *Interwoven.*" *Texas Monthly*, November 1999, 24.

"Movie of the Century: *Giant.*" *Texas Monthly*, December 1999, 144, 179.

"Actor of the Century: Sissy Spacek." *Texas Monthly*, December 1999, 144.

"Don Graham's Texas Classics: *North Dallas Forty.*" *Texas Monthly,* December 1999, 28.
"Lone Star Literature." In *Celebrating the Literary Heritage of Texas,* 5–11. Prentice-Hall: Upper Saddle River, N.J., 1999.
"Lone Star Life on Screen: Texas in the Movies." In *Celebrating the Literary Heritage of Texas,* 82–87. Prentice-Hall: Upper Saddle River, N.J. 1999.

2000

"Don Graham's Texas Classics: *George Washington Gómez.*" *Texas Monthly,* January 2000, 26.
"Deep in the Heart of Texas." *American Movie Classics,* February 2000, 4–6.
"Don Graham's Texas Classics: *Goodbye to a River.*" *Texas Monthly,* February 2000, 26.
"Wayne's World." *Texas Monthly,* March 2000, 108–113, 144–145.
"Don Graham's Texas Classics: *Viva Max!*" *Texas Monthly,* March 2000, 28.
"Don Graham's Texas Classics: *The Log of a Cowboy.*" *Texas Monthly,* April 2000, 24.
"Don Graham's Texas Classics: *Texas Music Movies.*" *Texas Monthly,* May 2000, 24.
"Ghosts and Empty Sockets" [fiction]. *Southwestern American Literature* 25.2 (Spring 2000), 51–57.
"Texas Classics: J. Frank Dobie." *Texas Bound,* Spring/Summer 2000, 32.
"Don Graham's Texas Classics: *The Time It Never Rained.*" *Texas Monthly,* June 2000, 22.
"Don Graham's Texas Classics: *My First Thirty Years.*" *Texas Monthly,* July 2000, 22.
"Don Graham's Texas Classics: *My Confession: Recollections of a Rogue.*" *Texas Monthly,* August 2000, 26.
"Don Graham's Texas Classics: *Blood Meridian.*" *Texas Monthly,* September 2000, 28.
"The Pits." *Texas Monthly,* October 2000, 70, 72, 74.
"Don Graham's Texas Classics: *Alpaca.*" *Texas Monthly,* October 2000, 26.
"Don Graham's Texas Classics: *Strange Peaches.*" *Texas Monthly,* November 2000, 28.

"Don Graham's Texas Classics: *Confessions of a Washed-Up Sportswriter.*" *Texas Monthly*, December 2000, 28.

"Oil Field Girls" [fiction]. In *Texas Short Stories 2*, ed. Billy Bob Hill & Laurie Champion (Dallas: Browder Springs Books, 2000), 837–839.

"Lone Star Life on Screen: Texas in the Movies." In *The Texas Experience: Arrivals and Departures in Literature* (Upper Saddle River, N.J.: Prentice Hall, 2000), 217–221.

"Texas Literary Traditions: The Voices of Texas." In *Prentice Hall Literature/Timeless Voices, Timeless Themes: Gold Level* (Upper Saddle River, N.J.: Prentice Hall, 2000), Tx2–Tx5.

"Texas Literary Traditions: The Uniqueness of Texas." *Prentice Hall Literature/Timeless Voices, Timeless Themes: Platinum Level* (Upper Saddle River, N.J.: Prentice Hall, 2000), Tx2–Tx5.

"Texas Connection: The Cowboy: The Last Cavalier." *Prentice Hall Literature/Timeless Voices, Timeless Themes: The British Tradition* (Upper Saddle River, N.J.: Prentice Hall, 2000), A6.

"Texas Connection: Shakespeare in Texas." *Prentice Hall Literature/Timeless Voices, Timeless Themes: The British Tradition* (Upper Saddle River, N.J.: Prentice Hall, 2000), A9.

"Texas Connection: Alexander Pope and Statesmen in Early Texas." *Prentice Hall Literature/Timeless Voices, Timeless Themes: The British Tradition* (Upper Saddle River, N.J.: Prentice Hall, 2000), A16.

"Texas Connection: A British Modernist in Texas." *Prentice Hall Literature/Timeless Voices, Timeless Themes: The British Tradition* (Upper Saddle River, N.J.: Prentice Hall, 2000), A40.

2001

"Don Graham's Texas Classics: *A Prince of a Fellow.*" *Texas Monthly*, January 2001, 24.

"Don Graham's Texas Classics: *The Perfect Sonya.*" *Texas Monthly*, February 2001, 22.

"Don Graham's Texas Classics: *. . . And the Earth Did Not Devour Him.*" *Texas Monthly*, March 2001, 26.

"Knightmare." *Texas Monthly*, April 2001, 113–114, 116.

"Writers Bloc: Fifty Great Literary Moments in Texas." *Texas Monthly*, May 2001, 132–137.

"Belles Lettres Blues." *The Texas Observer*, May 11, 2001, 24–25.

"The Write Brothers." *Texas Monthly,* August 2001, 132, 171–172.
"*Dallas:* Oil's Final Triumph in Texas Mythology." *The Texas Gulf Historical and Biographical Record* 37.2 (November 2001), 5966.
"Catcher in the Raw." *Texas Monthly,* December 2001, 116, 118, 120.
"Katherine Anne Porter's Journey from Texas to the World." In *From Texas to the World and Back,* ed. Mark Busby & Dick Heaberlin (Fort Worth: TCU Press, 2001), 1–19.

2002

"Now That's Comedy (Texas' Funniest Movies)." *Texas Monthly,* January 22, 2002 (online).
"Mission: Impossible." *Texas Monthly,* February 2002, 83–85.
"Giant." *Texas Monthly,* May 2002, 128–130.
"King Ranch: The Secret History" [cover story]. *Texas Monthly,* December 2002, 116–121, 198, 200–201.
"Ranch Undressing." texasmonthly.com/mag/issues/2002-12-01/webextra2.php?1153287263

2003

"Master Class." *Texas Monthly,* January 2003, 123–125.
"*Kings of Texas:* A Conversation with Don Graham." Interview by Dick Holland. *Texas Books in Review* 23.1 (Spring 2003), 12–15.
"Court Corrals a King Ranch Family Feud." *San Antonio Express-News,* May 4, 2003, H1, H6.
"Not Moving On." *Texas Monthly,* May 2003, 84, 86, 103.
Profile of Don Graham: "The Landscape, the Accents, and the Sky." By Peter Partheymuller. *The Alcalde,* May/June 2003, 44–47.
"Not-So-Great Plains." *Texas Monthly,* October 2003, 74, 76, 78, 80. [Reprinted in *Contemporary Literary Criticism* 250 (2008).]
"Tall in the Saddle." *San Antonio Express-News,* November 30, 2003, H1.
"King of Texas: An Interview with Don Graham." *Austin Chronicle,* November 7, 2003, 38.
"Alamo Heights" [cover story]. *Texas Monthly,* December 2003, 132, 144, 214, 216, 218, 220, 234.
"The Critic" [interview]. *Texas Monthly,* online, December, 2003.

Kings of Texas: The 150-Year Saga of an American Ranching Empire (Hoboken, N.J.: John Wiley & Sons, 2003).

(Ed.) *Lone Star Literature: From the Red River to the Rio Grande* (New York: W. W. Norton, 2003).

2004

"The Texas Literary Hall of Fame." *Texas Books in Review* 24.1 (Spring 2004), 12–15.

"Past the Hat: Interview with Don Graham." *Dallas Morning News,* March 14, 2004, G1, G4.

"Nation State." *Texas Monthly,* March 2004, 100, 102–103.

"Lit, Crit, 'N Grits: Interview with Don Graham." Interview by James McWilliams. *The Texas Observer,* April 9, 2004, 6–8.

"Expatriate Act." *Texas Monthly,* May 2004, 104, 108, 110.

"White Like Me." *Texas Monthly,* August 2004, 78, 80–81.

"Accentuate the Negative." *Texas Monthly,* November 2004, 98, 102, 117.

"The State of Texas Lit." *The Texas Observer* 96.23 (December 4, 2004), 24–25.

2005

"Mary, Quite Contrary." *Texas Monthly,* May 2005, 102, 104, 106, 108.

"The Confessional" [online interview]. *Texas Monthly,* http://texas monthly.printthis.clickability.com/ptcpt?action=cpt&title=Texas+ Monthly+May.

"All the Pretty Corpses." *Texas Monthly,* August 2005, 78, 95, 97.

"You've Got Mailer." *Texas Monthly,* November 2005, 94, 96, 105, 108.

2006

"Two Women Look West." *Texas Monthly,* February 2006, 25.

"Owens Country." *The Texas Observer* 96.4 (February 24, 2006), 29–31.

"Zane Grey's Texas—And Mine." *Desert Candle* 3.10 (Summer 2006), 6–8.

"Who Wrote *A Vaquero of the Brush Country?* A Strange Case of

Demoted Authorship." *Southwest American Literature* 32.1 (Fall 2006), 71–77.
"Let's Hear It for Cormac." *Texas Books in Review* 25.3–4 (Fall/Winter 2005–2006), 9–10.

2007

"Dunces of Confederacy." *Texas Monthly,* July 2007, 82, 84, 86.
"Texas Book Festival Bookend Award: A Tribute to Rolando Hinojosa-Smith." *Texas Books in Review* 28.4 (Winter 2007–2008), 6.
(Ed.) *Literary Austin* (Fort Worth: TCU Press, 2007).
"Mug's Game: *Literary Austin* edited by Don Graham." *Texas Books in Review* 27, 4 (Winter 2007–2008), 7, 18.
"Auroras of Autumn: John Graves' Valediction." In *John Graves, Writer,* edited by Mark Busby and Terrell Dixon. Austin: University of Texas Press, 2007, 225–236.
"Mission Statement: The Alamo and the Fallacy of Historical Accuracy in Epic Filmmaking." In *Lone Star Pasts: Memory and History in Texas,* edited by Gregg Cantrell and Elizabeth Hayes Turner. College Station: Texas A&M Press, 2007, 242–269.

2008

"Deathless Prose." *Texas Observer* 100.3 (February 8, 2008), 29–31.
"Please Go Away: An Open Letter to Cormac McCarthy." *Texas Monthly,* July 2008, 96, 98, 100–101.
"Nine Ball, Corner Pocket." In *Notes from Texas: On Writing in the Lone Star State,* ed. W. C. Jameson (Fort Worth: TCU Press, 2008), 46–61.
"Lone Star Cinema: A Century of Texas in the Movies." In *Twentieth-Century Texas: A Social and Cultural History,* eds. John W. Storey and Mary L. Kelley. Denton: University of North Texas Press, 2008, 245–266.
"Prayer on the Prairie: Texas Writers and the Question of Religion." *Langdon Review of the Arts in Texas* 5 (2008), 162–171.
State Fare: An Irreverent Guide to Texas Movies. (Fort Worth: TCU Press, 2008).

2009

"*Brokeback Mountain* in My Rear-view Mirror." *Southwestern American Literature* 34.2 (Spring 2009), 45–51.
"One Day in Dallas." *The Texas Observer,* March 6, 2009, 26–27.
"On Texas Culture: Big Texas Towers and Little Texas Poetry." *The Alcalde* 98.1 (September/October 2009), 14.

CREDITS

"The State of Texas Lit," *The Texas Observer* 96.23 (December 4, 2004), pp. 24–25. Courtesy of Brad Tyer, Managing Editor.

"*Brokeback Mountain* in My Rear-View Mirror," *Southwestern American Literature* 34.2 (Spring 2009), pp. 45–51. Courtesy of Mark Busby, Coeditor.

"*Dallas:* Oil's Final Triumph in Texas Mythology," *The Texas Gulf Historical and Biographical Record* 37.2 (November 2001), pp. 59–66. Courtesy of Curtis Leister, President of the Board of the Texas Gulf Historical & Biographical Society.

"Owens Country," *The Texas Observer* 96.4 (February 24, 2006), pp. 29–31. Courtesy of Brad Tyer, Managing Editor.

"White Like Me," *Texas Monthly,* August 2004, pp. 78, 80–81. Courtesy of Cathy S. Casey, Senior Editor (Special Projects), *Texas Monthly.*

"Cotton Tale," *Texas Monthly,* May 1999, pp. 108, 110, 112, 116. Courtesy of Cathy S. Casey, Senior Editor (Special Projects), *Texas Monthly.*

"Catcher in the Raw," *Texas Monthly,* December 2001, pp. 115, 118, 120. Courtesy of Cathy S. Casey, Senior Editor (Special Projects), *Texas Monthly.*

"Master Class," *Texas Monthly,* January 2003, pp. 123–125. Courtesy of Cathy S. Casey, Senior Editor (Special Projects), *Texas Monthly.*

"Fallen Heroes," *Texas Monthly,* February 2005, pp. 70, 83–85. Courtesy of Cathy S. Casey, Senior Editor (Special Projects), *Texas Monthly.*

"The Pits," *Texas Monthly,* October 2001, pp. 70, 72, 74. Courtesy of Cathy S. Casey, Senior Editor (Special Projects), *Texas Monthly.*

"Accentuate the Negative," *Texas Monthly,* November 2004, pp. 98, 102, 117. Courtesy of Cathy S. Casey, Senior Editor (Special Projects), *Texas Monthly.*

"Expatriate Act," *Texas Monthly,* May 2004, pp. 104, 108, 110. Courtesy of Cathy S. Casey, Senior Editor (Special Projects), *Texas Monthly.*

"Nation State," *Texas Monthly,* March 2004, pp. 100, 101–103. Courtesy of Cathy S. Casey, Senior Editor (Special Projects), *Texas Monthly.*

"The Write Brothers," *Texas Monthly,* August 2001, pp. 132, 171–172. Courtesy of Cathy S. Casey, Senior Editor (Special Projects), *Texas Monthly.*

"All the Pretty Corpses," *Texas Monthly,* August 2005, pp. 78, 93, 97. Courtesy of Cathy S. Casey, Senior Editor (Special Projects), *Texas Monthly.*

"Wayne's World," *Texas Monthly,* March 2000, pp. 108–113, 145–146. Courtesy of Cathy S. Casey, Senior Editor (Special Projects), *Texas Monthly.*

"Picture Perfect: The Making of *The Last Picture Show,*" *Texas Monthly,* February 1999, pp. 72–80, 100–111. Courtesy of Cathy S. Casey, Senior Editor (Special Projects), *Texas Monthly.*

"Giant," *Texas Monthly,* May 2002, pp. 128–130. Courtesy of Cathy S. Casey, Senior Editor (Special Projects), *Texas Monthly.*

"Please Go Away," *Texas Monthly,* July 2008, pp. 96, 98, 100–101. Courtesy of Cathy S. Casey, Senior Editor (Special Projects), *Texas Monthly.*

"Zane Grey's Texas—and Mine," *Desert Candle* 3.10 (Summer 2006), pp. 6–8. Courtesy of *Desert Candle.*

"Let's Hear It for Cormac," *Texas Books in Review* 25.3–4 (Fall/Winter 2005–2006), pp. 9–10. Courtesy of Mark Busby, Southwest Regional Humanities Center, Texas State University.

"Nine Ball, Corner Pocket," in *Notes from Texas: On Writing in the Lone Star State,* ed. W. C. Jameson (Fort Worth: TCU Press, 2008), pp. 46–61. Courtesy of Susan Petty, TCU Press.